THE

ENGLISH

LIBRARY

General Editor JAMES SUTHERLAND

Emeritus Professor of Modern Literature
University College, London

THE
TRIBE OF BEN

Pre-Augustan Classical Verse in English

Edited by
A. C. PARTRIDGE

Professor of English, University of the Witwatersrand, Johannesburg

UNIVERSITY OF SOUTH CAROLINA PRESS
Columbia, S.C.

Published 1966 in Great Britain by
EDWARD ARNOLD (PUBLISHERS) LTD.
41 Maddox Street, London W.1

Published 1970 in the United States of America by the
UNIVERSITY OF SOUTH CAROLINA PRESS
Columbia, S.C. 29208

Standard Book Number: 87249-159-5
Library of Congress Catalog Card Number: 75-116473

Manufactured in Great Britain

General Preface

THE design of this series is to present fully annotated selections from English literature which will, it is hoped, prove satisfactory both in their breadth and their depth. To achieve this, some of the volumes have been planned so as to provide a varied selection from the poetry or prose of a limited period, which is both long enough to have developed a literary movement, and short enough to allow for adequate representation of the chief writers and of the various cross-currents within the movement. Examples of such periods are the late seventeenth century and the early eighteenth century. In other volumes the principle of selection is to present a literary kind (e.g. satirical poetry, the literary ballad). Here it is possible to cover a longer period without sacrificing the unified and comprehensive treatment which is the governing idea for the whole series. Other volumes, again, are designed to present a group of writers who form some kind of "school" (e.g. the Elizabethan sonneteers, the followers of Ben Jonson), or who were closely enough linked for their work to be brought together (e.g. the poetry of Johnson and Goldsmith).

Each volume has a full critical introduction. Headnotes, a special feature of this series, provide relevant background and critical comment for the individual poems and prose pieces. The footnotes are for the most part explanatory, giving as briefly as possible information about persons, places, allusions of one kind or another, the meaning of words, etc., which the twentieth-century reader is likely to require. Each selection aims at providing examples of the best work of the authors represented, but it is hoped that the inclusion of some less familiar pieces not available in any other collection will widen the reader's experience and enjoyment of the literature under review. The series is intended for use in universities and the upper forms of schools.

For most twentieth-century readers English poetry of the seventeenth century means the poetry of Donne and Herbert and the other metaphysical poets. In this volume, which ranges from the mid-sixteenth century to near the close of the seventeenth century, Professor Partridge has made a selection from those poets who, "in favouring certain forms and themes, and in the urbanity and direct-ness of their expression", achieved a true English classicism before the neo-classical period of Dryden and Pope. This earlier classicism had all the diversity of Greek and Latin poetry, but was entirely English in its themes and in its plain, idiomatic style of writing. Avoiding "metaphors far-fet" and aiming at perspicuity and "pure and neat language", Jonson, Raleigh, Campion, the Milton of the minor poems, Herrick, Waller, Denham, Cowley and many others wrote poetry which was often essentially classical in its interpreta-tion and expression. Even such poets as Marvell and Carew, who are usually thought of as metaphysicals, come within Professor Partridge's terms of definition, and add to the diversity and interest of his selection. This volume makes available a kind of poetry which was not only widely written in the seventeenth century, but which deserves on its own merits to be as well known and carefully studied as that of the metaphysical poets.

Contents

Introduction

IN the eighteenth century "Baroque" and "Metaphysical" were terms of disparagement; in the twentieth they have become names of important developments in the plastic and literary arts. The movement called "Augustanism" shows this process in reverse; for it once was conceived as the pinnacle of English classicism, yet as early as 1800 had fallen into the kind of disfavour from which it is difficult to recover.

Augustanism in England is usually thought to begin with Dryden and to culminate in Pope. The purpose of this anthology is to suggest that the English classical tendency in verse put forth its "tender leaves of hope" in the reign of Henry VIII. In the period 1590 to 1650 it was naturalized to the vernacular aspirations of English speech, first by Ben Jonson, then by John Milton. While there is no real *school* of classical poetry in England before Jonson, there was a tradition of gnomic, aphoristic poetry, in the plain style, that sprang from Chaucer, Skelton, Heywood and Wyatt. The style was cultivated in the complaints and expostulations of Sir Walter Raleigh, as well as in the ballads of the song-writers, and given an impetus by the expository prose of George Gascoigne and Francis Bacon.

The verse of Jonson and his pre-Restoration followers is related in spirit and content to that of the Greek and Roman poets—more to the latter, because there was a smaller proportion of Greek to Latin scholars. Dryden, Pope and Dr. Johnson narrowed the range and appeal of Augustan poetry by confining it to couplets of ten or eleven syllables, self-contained epigrams with a nicely balanced or antithetical structure. Jonson's classicism was a new creation in English and his *Discoveries* a statement of classical ideals more attractive in individuality than Pope's *Essay on Criticism*, which borrows its shibboleths of correctness from Horace, Vida and Boileau. French classicism, summarized in *L'Art Poétique*, suffered from the dubious virtue of Cartesian intelligence and formality. Descartes was thus indirectly a founder of the Royal Society, and his *Discourses on Method* had something to do with the dominance in Augustan poetry of Latin rules over Greek flexibility. The homogeneity of the Gallic classical spirit springs from the genius of the language. In its taste for elegance, propriety and the *mot juste*, it is a product of Roman civilization.

The beginnings of the Anglo-classical literary movement are to be found in the work of the humanist intellectuals, Erasmus, Sir Thomas More,

Roger Ascham, Sir John Cheke and Richard Mulcaster. More's typically English humour was more congenial to the Greek, Lucian, than the Roman, Horace. Roger Ascham resented the foppery of the later Italianate invasion; and he found allies in those stout defenders of homely vigorous English, Sir John Cheke, Richard Mulcaster and Ben Jonson. These men successfully grafted the classical tradition on to the English one, and gave to English humanism a language refined, dignified, and resourceful, that was to dominate the thinking of the first half of the seventeenth century. Jonson claimed that the ancient authors were "guides", not "commanders"; he persuaded his "Sons" to prefer the good sense of Quintilian to the florid periods of Cicero; and he favoured those forms of poetry—lyric, satiric and gratulatory—in which the epigram, in its diversity, could best be utilized.

The draught of Renaissance thinking that came from Sidney and Spenser was filtered through Neo-Platonism. In style they were of the Alexandrian school, and closer to Apuleius, Ovid and the mediaeval Latinists, than to the salty wit and concision of Catullus, Horace and Martial. The conversational style of Horace's *sermones* (self-revealing discourses) Jonson found to be best for his sinewy intellectualism. Like Bacon, he distrusted the flamboyance and extravagance of "Asiatic" rhetoric. His epigrams, tributes and mono-logues are Socratic and Senecan in their candour and concern for virtue as an activity of the rational mind. His style has the directness recommended by Demetrius; and he was the first writer in modern English to perceive that the word order of good speech needs no modification for the purposes of either verse or prose. He aimed at a style that would be a model for younger writers, believing that Spenser, Donne and Shakespeare (of the 'sugred sonnets") were not in the highway of any English tradition. The object of Jonson's epistolary style is to ensure intimacy between the poet and the reader.

The ancient philosophers and critics agreed with Horace that poetry should instruct as well as delight; in their pagan culture it assumed many of the functions of religion. The most Greek of English poets, Milton and Shelley, thought likewise. Poetry intended to edify looks to the art of persuasion, which is not static but experimental. Latin poets from Horace to Martial wrote no longer for speaking, as Plautus did, but for the cultivated reader; and their verse began to differ materially from Greek poetry. The lyrical poets of *The Greek Anthology* composed for musical accompaniment; to this end their verse was dynamic in rhythm, and popular in appeal. Formal classifications of Greek poetry belong to the Alexandrian era, when scholars founded them on metrical principles, subject-matter and treatment —a utilitarian arrangement that might have seemed strange to Aristotle.

The doctrine of 'kinds' blunted the impact of classical poets upon Western European literature. The importance of Catullus lies not in his forms, but his fugitive delights, his mingled playfulness and seriousness.

Jonson's conviction that poetry, like prose, should enlighten pervades his humanistic conception of literature. The value of his observations on writing in *Discoveries* is their practical application; for criticism in the English Renaissance was mainly theoretical, and sometimes in conflict with the poet-critic's practice. The closeness of the poetry and prose is characteristic of classical eras, because the ideal of the written language is refined conversation. Jonson set down the principles of style clearly in *Discoveries*; a few are worth recording, to illustrate the authority of Aristotle, Horace and Quintilian on his critical judgment:

XIX   A man should so deliver himself to the nature of the subject whereof he speaks, that his hearer may take knowledge of his discipline with some delight; and so apparel fair and good matter, that the studious of elegancy be not defrauded; redeem arts from their rough and braky seats, where they lay hid and over-grown with thorns, to a pure, open and flow'ry light, where they may take the eye, and be taken by the hand.

LXV   The true artificer will not run away from Nature as he were afraid of her, or depart from life and the likeness of truth, but speak to the capacity of his hearers. . . . He knows it is his only art so to carry it, as none but artificers perceive it. . . . Then in his elocution to behold what word is proper, which hath ornament, which height, what is beautifully translated [i.e. expressed in metaphor], where figures fit, which gentle, which strong, to show the composition manly; and how he hath avoided faint, obscure, obscene, sordid, humble, improper or effeminate phrase.

CXV   . . . the safest is to return to our judgment, and handle over again those things the easiness of which might make them justly suspected. So did the best writers in their beginnings; they imposed upon themselves care and industry; they did nothing rashly; they obtained first to write well, and the custom made it easy and a habit. By little and little their matter showed itself to them more plentifully; their words answered, their composition followed; and all, as in a well-ordered family, presented itself in place.

CXVIII   . . . out of the observation, knowledge, and the use of things, many writers perplex their readers and hearers with mere nonsense. Their writings need sunshine. Pure and neat language

I love, yet plain and customary. A barbarous phrase hath often made me out of love with a good sense, and doubtful [i.e. ambiguous] writing hath wracked me beyond my patience.

CXIX In all speech, words and sense are the body and the soul. The sense is as the life and soul of language, without which all words are dead. Sense is wrought out of experience, the knowledge of human life and actions, or of the liberal arts. . . . Metaphors far-fet [i.e. fetched] hinder to be understood; and affected, lose their grace . . . the chief virtue of a style is perspicuity, and nothing so vicious in it as to need an interpreter. Words borrowed of antiquity do lend a kind of majesty to style, and are not without their delight sometimes; for they have the authority of years, and out of their intermission do win themselves a kind of gracelike newness. . . . Some words are to be culled out for ornament and colour, as we gather flowers to straw [i.e. strew] houses and make garlands; but they are better when they grow to our style. . . . A strict and succinct style is that where you can take away nothing without loss, and that loss to be manifest.

CXX Our style should be like a skein of silk, to be carried and found by the right thread, not ravelled and perplexed.

CXXIII Nothing is more ridiculous than to make an author a dictator, as the schools have done Aristotle.

CXXX It is said of the incomparable Virgil that he brought forth his verses like a bear, and after formed them with licking. . . . The poet is the nearest borderer upon the orator, and expresseth all his virtues, though he be tied more to numbers, is his equal in ornament, and above him in his strengths.

With all his burly independence, Jonson was a traditionalist, like T. S. Eliot, but in some of his pronouncements he gave the impression of being a rebel. His taste in style does not extend to Latinized vocabulary and syntax, except on the most formal occasions; for he says good writing should be "plain and customary", meaning that it should resemble the speech of learned men versed in Greek and Roman authors. Despite his preference for Latin models, however, he is English in his individuality, without being insular. No one knew better that Pindar and Horace were inimitable, because the genius, tone and inflexions of their languages were different. The modulations of classical poetry were not possible in an uninflected vernacular, whose character was rooted in the custom of stressed syllables. Marlowe's *Hero and Leander* and Chapman's Homer were successful in English because the translators became adapters eager to create something new. Phaer's Vergil and Golding's Ovid were, on the other hand, period pieces. In prose, North's Plutarch and Holland's Pliny attracted the discriminating on account of the uninhibited freedom of their versions.

According to Drummond, Jonson "had written a discourse of Poesie both against Campion and Daniel . . . where he proves couplets to be the bravest sort of verses, especially when they are broken, like hexameters, and that cross-rhymes and stanzas [because the purpose would lead him beyond eight lines to conclude] were all forced." Campion's Greek classifications for English poetry in his *Observations in the Art of English Poesy*, in fact, contain tongue-in-the-cheek statements about rhyme that are refuted by his practice. His classical measures in English call to mind Thomas Nashe's remarks on imitations of Greek hexameters:

> The Hexamiter verse I graunt to be a Gentleman of an auncient house (so is many an english begger), yet this Clyme of ours hee cannot thrive in; our speech is too craggy for him to set his plough in; hee goes twitching and hopping in our language like a man running upon quagmiers, up the hill in one Syllable, and down the dale in another, retaining no part of that stately smooth gate which he vaunts himselfe with amongst the Greeks and Latins.

On the other hand, Campion's songs in rhyme are among the finest of Elizabethan lyrics, and prove how indispensable rhyme is to English lyrical metres. The threadbare arguments that invalidate it are amusingly stated in Jonson's "Fit of Rime against Rime".

From Catullus to Martial, Latin poetry is mainly in pairs of verses called epigrams, confining the sense to the distich. This became the staple metre of a number of forms not strictly lyrical, but adopted because the epigram had been so effectively used in the Greek *Garland* of Meleager. Jonson appreciated the epigram's flexibility, and he used it for Eulogies, Epitaphs, Epistles and miniature Satires. His subtly paused diction studied to suit the syntax to the rhythm, in the style of Horace, whether he wrote odes, hymns, or discursive and topographical poems. Horace seemed to him the complete humanist, to whom poetry was a way of life, enjoining balance and self-knowledge.

The earlier English poets in the epigrammatic style, Wyatt, Raleigh and Southwell, had not Jonson's skill in versification. This mastery separates him equally from Donne. Donne's love poetry may resemble Jonson's in its anti-Petrarchan feeling; but his reading had led him to different Latin, mediaeval and Renaissance sources, to Lucretius, Tertullian, St. Augustine, Aquinas, Dante and du Bartas. In philosophical learning Donne was deeper than Jonson, who preferred the fashionable western European blend of

Stoicism and Epicureanism. It was Donne's personality and logical tenacity of conceit that saved him from the vices of style that eventually killed the metaphysical movement in the eighteenth century.

Jonson and Donne were born within a year of each other; they knew and admired each other's work, moved in the same literary society, and circulated most of their poems privately. Jonson's first Epigrams were printed in the Folio of 1616; but Donne's poems were not published until 1633, and his influence was, therefore, the more tardy. There was no "School of Donne" until the second quarter of the seventeenth century; but the impact of Jonson, through drama upon poetry, was noticeable by 1600. The different reputations of the two poets for learning and colloquial language were reconciled by conceding that Donne was the greater "wit" (the meaning of "invention" or "play of mind" seems to derive from Quintilian), and Jonson the surer artist. Donne did not think of himself as a professional poet, and made few pronouncements about his art. As Grierson observed, Donne lacked "the two essentials of 'classical' poetry—smoothness of verse and dignity of expression". His feeling and thought were more often in conflict than communion.

The best of Donne's poetry belonged to his early twenties; but the most perfect of Jonson's non-dramatic poems were the fruit of middle age. The presence of images as generators of poetic energy is not the distinguishing mark of classical poets; but the infrequency of conceits in epistles and devotional poems is noticeable even in Donne. What stamps Donne is the intellectual turn of mind, the fantasy of wit, the alternating mood of gay paradox and melancholy scepticism. The devotional hymns *To God the Father* illustrate the different expressions of piety and humanism in the two poets.

The qualities Donne and Jonson share are masculinity, integrity, command of pungent epigram and a preference for natural rhythms of speech. Donne draws upon mythological machinery less than Jonson. The tone of both is urbane, and their songs are unmelodious. If Jonson's can more easily be set to music, it is because they are simpler in rhythm and vocabulary. The lyrical "Sons of Ben" of the Commonwealth and Restoration made lucidity, neatness and point the aims of their style. Only Waller, Denham and Dryden improved upon the couplet as a dialectical instrument.

Jonson and Donne are best distinguished by the movement and forms of their verse. In Donne the form is tied to the subtle progression of thought; the movement follows the sense, intonation and emphasis of living utterance. The facility of Jonson results from disciplined habits of composition; his tone in serious poetry is public and formal. He told Drummond that his master, William Camden, had instructed him to draft all his verse first in prose; and this may explain the meticulous filing and retrenchment of phrase. Horace's *Art of Poetry*, translated, is the least successful of Jonson's verse discourses, because it is no more than a careful rendering.

Paradoxical and discordant wit is less visible in Jonson than in Donne; he is impersonal and controlled, where Donne is individual and outspoken. George Williamson in *The Proper Wit of Poetry* says of Jonson's "unemphatic tone" that "even in hyperbole [he] tried to suggest the politeness of understatement". Jonson worked best on a small scale, in language that was clear, concentrated and forceful.

A classical poem characteristic of Jonson and his followers has the following qualities:

1. It does not make self-expression or imaginative inspiration a principle of art.
2. It seeks to preserve the matter, diction and traditional forms of poetry, the thing said being less important than the manner of saying it.
3. The language is urbane, often sophisticated; the choice of words moderate, masculine and unadorned. The related style in prose is distinguished by simplicity, lucidity and spareness.
4. Paradox, antithesis, understatement, climax and irony are employed more vigorously than metaphor and metonymy. In the narrative and discursive poems the sustained simile of Greek and Roman epic is often introduced.
5. Except in lyrics, the intellectual content is more important than sentiment or feeling.
6. The memorable songs are short, well balanced and restrained in evocative emotion. Campion says in his note to the reader (*A Book of Airs*, 1601): "What epigrams are in poetry, the same are airs in music . . . in their chief perfection when they are short and well seasoned."
7. Except in Pindaric odes, the stanza forms are simple; unity and succinctness, by progression in couplets, is preferred to quatrains with alternate rhymes, which are the staple of church hymns.
8. Reflective poems have a moral tone, and the philosophy is usually Stoical or Epicurean, or a synthesis of both. Self-analysis, ending in resignation such as Raleigh's, owes much to Boethius's *Consolations of Philosophy* and the choruses of Seneca's plays (see Godolphin's "Vain man, born to no happiness").

Robert Frost defined poetry as "that which gets lost from verse and prose in translation". He was speaking of those overtones of poetic expressions that cannot be transposed. This volume contains no translations except Jonson's epistle, based on Martial, and Cowley's free adaptation of Horace on Pindar. These poems transmute their models in a creative way. It may be that Jonson does not assimilate borrowings from the classics as functionally as Shakespeare in his use of Ovid; but his knowledge of the classics was greater. He set himself to school with Aristotle, Longinus, Quintilian, Catullus, Horace, the two Senecas, Martial and others. But the innovation of Jonson was to seize upon the spirit, not the form. He taught the art of fruitful imitation to Cowley, Dryden, Pope, Cowper and subsequent verse translators, some of whom outdistanced their originals. Jonson understood the *raison d'être* of a humanist education, which, as H. A. Mason pointed out, is "as much a matter of living as of writing" (*Humanism and Poetry in the Early Tudor Period*). Consequently the poems in this book are not chosen as specimens of the highest poetic art; they illustrate a certain line of development before Dryden that seems in need of further exploration, and that can be seen in embryo as early as Wyatt. Hence the inclusion of some pre-Jonson poems.

A few selections in this anthology may occasion surprise; for instance, sonnets of Milton. In the three chosen, Milton pours into an Italian mould the dignified expression of an epistle of Horace. In the same way, the two topographical poems, "To Penshurst" and "To Saxham", owe their inspiration to Theocritus, Horace, Vergil and Martial; but they are not merely versions of pastoral. These encomiums that set the fashion for Marvell, Carew, Herrick, Waller, Denham, Pope, Gray, Shenstone and Thomson, are expressions of another side of the humanist tradition, gracious living at the country seats of noblemen. For much of classical poetry is devoted to "the good life", to hospitality and the social pursuits of the leisured class. The great homes became centres of regional culture, and Sir Philip Sidney was, no doubt, the source of such idealism in Elizabethan poetry. The taste for rural culture was developed by arboriculturists like John Evelyn in the seventeenth century, and the celebration of English folk festivals by cheerful parsons like Robert Herrick. The community spirit is finer in attitude to the local peasants than what we glean from Horace's unsympathetic epistle to the foreman on his Sabine estate. It is an error to suppose that classical poetry in any European language is devoid of a sensitive appreciation of nature.

In favouring certain forms and themes, and in the urbanity and directness of their expression, the Sons of Ben are a related group. The most important are Marvell, Carew and King (who have a foot in the metaphysical camp), Herrick and Waller. After 1650, new critical approaches to the language of poetry were adumbrated by Davenant and Hobbes, a dramatist of limited talent and a philosopher who tried to clear the linguistic air for science. Hobbes spoke of the "ambitious obscurity" of poets who express more than can be conceived; and Dryden soon diminished Jonsonian strength to a bloodless propriety. The authority of these critical potentates was immense, and the prestige of the Royal Society was behind them. After weeding out conceits, the Augustan poets planted, with scholastic zeal, the Russell-like tautologies of periphrasis. Images once more became Spenserian, decorative and not functional; wit an offensive weapon, not, as it was with Donne, integral to the texture of poetry. The opposition of Waller and Dryden is to Donne, not to Jonson. In fact, Augustanism was partly an attempt to eliminate the coloured strands of metaphysical conceit from the variegated skein of Jonsonian classicism. Pope had become the Jesuit proselytizer of Augustanism.

The poems here chosen appear conveniently under a dozen heads, which helped as criteria for inclusion. Several of the poems appear in the anthologies of Metaphysical Poetry prepared by H. J. C. Grierson and Helen Gardner, four in both collections, namely Carew's song "Ask me no more", Marvell's "The Garden", Milton's "On Shakespeare" and King's "Contemplation upon Flowers". Helen Gardner's concept of a metaphysical poem is more tolerant than Professor Grierson's; for the purpose of her selection was apparently to bring a wider range of reading to the notice of university students. The texts of the poems are from the earliest available old-spelling editions, the source being indicated in the headnotes. Italics have not been retained unless they are emphatic; the old u (e.g. giue), v (e.g. vpon), and i (e.g. iustice) have been altered to v, u, j, to conform with modern usage.

The compilation of an anthology such as this convinces one that classicism is not one thing, but many. The humanist poetry published in England between 1550 and 1650 had the diversity of Greek and Latin poetry, which seldom displayed typological characteristics, such as appeared in the Augustanism of Dryden, Pope and Dr. Johnson. Ben Jonson and Donne, in demonstrating the native subtlety of the English tongue in a way more colloquial than Shakespeare or Milton, did not aim at Palladian classicism. Poetry written in defence of a critical theory, they knew, carries the seeds of its dissolution. As Stanley Burnshaw wrote in *The Poem Itself*: "Poems are not made of ideas, they are made of words . . . each affective phrase is a rhythmic metaphor."

Gratitude and acknowledgement are expressed for the wise guidance of the General Editor, Professor James Sutherland, and of Professor Robert Birley in helping with some of the historical notes.

EPIGRAMS

TUDOR and Stuart poets were better acquainted with Latin than Greek. They modelled their poems in spirit, content and style, rarely in form, on the Roman poets from 75 B.C. to A.D. 125, chiefly Catullus, Vergil, Horace, Ovid, Martial and Juvenal. Ben Jonson aspired to do in English what Lucretius, Catullus, Vergil and Horace had accomplished in adapting Greek measures to the Latin tongue; he naturalized, without actual imitation, the Graeco-Latin "qualities of control, modulation, clarity and beauty".

Jonson was not interested in the academic classification of poetry according to metrical principles, which Aristophanes of Byzantium had initiated at Alexandria. As Catullus adapted measures from the poets of *The Greek Anthology*, Alcaeus, Sappho, Meleager, Musaeus, Simonides and Anacreon, so Jonson learnt from the Latin poetry of the golden age. His epigrams he described as "the ripest of my studies".

Epigram found employment in every branch of Greek melic (or personal) poetry. Here the poet sang in his own voice, instead of composing speeches for characters in dramatic or epic poems. Epigrams, though they began as inscriptions on statues, tombs and shrines, were not simply pointed, pithy and dignified verse utterances. In Greece the term "epigram" was available also for occasional poems that dealt with human incidents and fugitive emotions. If any mode of expression was characteristic of it, it would comprise frankness, brevity and simplicity. Martial regularly employed epigrams for the less attractive business of lampoons, preferably with a sting in the tail. So epigram became, in the ages of decadent sophistication, the staple of satire. But this evolution was not evident in classical Greek lyric poetry.

Jonson used the epigram with Greek grace and delicacy, as well as with Latin astringency in miniature satires. His eulogies, epitaphs and epistles have Horace's dignity, poise and sincerity. But he was no less indebted to William Camden, his mentor, who thought the English surpassed other nations in their use of epigrams, which he described as "short and sweet poems, framed to praise and dispraise".

I. EULOGIES

THE English poetic eulogy began as a short, typically classical epigram, but was expanded by Jonson in the tribute to Shakespeare specially written for the First Folio. The other poets here represented (Herrick, Denham and Waller) are true Sons of Ben. Waller, in a different way from Donne, broke the Petrarchan convention, in which tributes to lovers were usually expressed in sonnet form. Both he and Denham widen the range and interest of poetic tributes, and continue the Jonsonian tradition of critical comment.

Ben Jonson

PLAYWRIGHT, poet, critic and creator of court masques, Jonson left monuments of classical scholarship in his tragedies *Sejanus* and *Catiline*, and his critical notes entitled *Timber, or Discoveries*. With Henry Porter and Chapman, he established the popularity of "humour" comedy. *Every Man in His Humour* (1598) and its successors were a reaction to romantic comedy and chronicle history. Jonson's conception of the function of the poet in society was as lofty as Milton's or Shelley's.

In the light of sentiments expressed in the Eulogies, the reader is reminded of Section LXXX of Jonson's *Discoveries*: "I could never think the study of wisdom confined only to the philosopher, or of piety to the divine, or of state to the politic; but that which can feign a commonwealth (which is the poet), can gown it with counsels, strengthen it with laws, correct it with judgments, inform it with religion and words, is all these. We do not require in him mere elocution or an excellent faculty in verse, but the exact knowledge of all virtues and their contraries, with ability to render the one loved, the other hated."

All the selections, except the tribute to Shakespeare, are from the collected "Epigrammes" published in the Jonson First Folio of 1616. The text used is that of Herford and Simspson's edition, Vol. VIII.

TO WILLIAM CAMDEN

CAMDEN, the antiquary (1551-1623), author of *Britannia* (1586), *Remains of a Greater Work concerning Britain* (1607) and *Annals of the Reign of Queen Elizabeth* (1615-27), was educated at St. Paul's School and Magdalen College, Oxford, and taught Jonson at Westminster School, of which he became headmaster in 1593. He was appointed Clarenceux King of Arms in 1597. Jonson dedicated *Every Man in his Humour* to him. This poem illustrates the common practice of confining the eulogy to fourteen lines, not in sonnet form, but in seven couplets.

Camden, most reverend head, to whom I owe
    All that I am in arts, all that I know,
(How nothing's that?) to whom my countrey owes
    The great renowne, and name wherewith shee goes.
5 Then thee the age sees not that thing more grave,
    More high, more holy, that shee more would crave.
What name, what skill, what faith hast thou in things!
    What sight in searching the most antique springs!
What weight, and what authoritie in thy speech!
10   Man scarse can make that doubt, but thou canst teach.
Pardon free truth, and let thy modestie,
    Which conquers all, be once over-come by thee.
Many of thine this better could, then I,
    But for their powers, accept my pietie.

5 *Then:* Than.   7 *things:* facts, historical events.

ON LUCY COUNTESSE OF BEDFORD

THE Countess (1581-1627), a daughter of Sir John Harrington, poet and translator, was a court beauty, lady-in-waiting to Queen Elizabeth and patroness of letters. Jonson addressed two other tributes to her, in which reference is made to her piety. She participated in his *Masque of Queens*, loved gardens and herself wrote poetry. Grierson suggests that she actually wrote Donne's "Death be not Proud".

This morning, timely rapt with holy fire,
    I thought to forme unto my zealous Muse,
What kinde of creature I could most desire,
    To honor, serve, and love; as Poets use.
5 I meant to make her faire, and free, and wise,
    Of greatest bloud, and yet more good then great;
I meant the day-starre should not brighter rise,
    Nor lend like influence from his lucent seat.
I meant shee should be curteous, facile, sweet,
10   Hating that solemne vice of greatnesse, pride;
I meant each softest vertue, there should meet,
    Fit in that softer bosome to reside.

9 *facile:* kindly, accessible.

Onely a learned, and a manly soule
 I purpos'd her; that should, with even powers,
15 The rock, the spindle, and the sheeres controule
 Of destinie, and spin her owne free houres.
Such when I meant to faine, and wish'd to see,
 My Muse bad, *Bedford* write, and that was shee.

15 *The rock, the spindle and the sheeres:* symbols of the Fates, Clotho, Lachesis and Atropos.

TO THE MEMORY OF MY BELOVED, THE AUTHOR MR. WILLIAM SHAKESPEARE: AND WHAT HE HATH LEFT US

THIS tribute was prefaced, with an invitation to the reader, to the First Folio of Shakespeare's collected plays (1623). Jonson was probably a literary adviser for this edition. It was one of the amplest and most generous of his gratulatory poems.

To draw no envy (Shakespeare) on thy name,
 Am I thus ample to thy Booke, and Fame:
While I confesse thy writings to be such,
 As neither Man, nor Muse, can praise too much.
5 'Tis true, and all mens suffrage. But these wayes
 Were not the paths I meant unto thy praise:
For seeliest Ignorance on these may light,
 Which, when it sounds at best, but eccho's right;
Or blinde Affection, which doth ne're advance
10 The truth, but gropes, and urgeth all by chance;
 Or crafty Malice, might pretend this praise,
 And thinke to ruine, where it seem'd to raise.
These are, as some infamous Baud, or Whore,
 Should praise a Matron. What could hurt her more?
15 But thou art proofe against them, and indeed
 Above th'ill fortune of them, or the need.
I, therefore will begin. Soule of the Age!
 The applause! delight! the wonder of our Stage!
My Shakespeare, rise; I will not lodge thee by
20 Chaucer, or Spenser, or bid Beaumont lye

7 *seeliest:* most ingenuous, simplest.   **13** *as:* as if.

A little further, to make thee a roome:
    Thou art a Moniment, without a tombe,
And art alive still, while thy Booke doth live,
    And we have wits to read, and praise to give.
25 That I not mixe thee so, my braine excuses;
    I meane with great, but disporportion'd Muses;
For, if I thought my judgement were of yeeres,
    I should commit thee surely with thy peeres,
And tell, how farre thou didst our Lily out-shine,
30   Or sporting Kid, or Marlowes mighty line.
And though thou hadst small Latine, and lesse Greeke,
    From thence to honour thee, I would not seeke
For names; but call forth thund'ring Æschilus,
    Euripides, and Sophocles to us,
35 Paccuvius, Accius, him of Cordova dead,
    To life againe, to heare thy Buskin tread,
And shake a State: Or, when thy Sockes were on,
    Leave thee alone, for the comparison
Of all, that insolent Greece, or haughtie Rome
40   Sent forth, or since did from their ashes come.
Triumph, my Britaine, thou hast one to showe,
    To whom all Scenes of Europe homage owe.

20-1 A reference to the fact that the three poets mentioned are buried in Westminster Abbey, though Shakespeare is not.

27 *of yeeres:* of sufficient historical authority.　　**28** *commit:* place.

29 *Lily:* John Lyly, Shakespeare's predecessor as playwright of court comedies, such as *Campaspe* and *Endimion*.

30 *Kid:* Thomas Kyd, author of *The Spanish Tragedy*, a revenge play that anticipates *Hamlet*. Jonson is supposed to have played Hieronomo in it. "Sporting" probably means "immature", rather than playful, and is a punning epithet associated with the name.

35 *Paccuvius, Accius:* early Roman tragedians, little of whose work survives.　　*him of Cordova dead:* Seneca the younger, a philosopher who was born in Spain, and became the most famous of Latin tragedians.

36 *Buskin:* the *kothornos* or square-toed boot worn by the actors, but not the chorus, in Greek tragedy.

37 *Sockes:* the low-heeled slippers (Roman *socci*) worn by the actors in Greek comedy.

42 *Scenes:* theatres.

He was not of an age, but for all time!
And all the Muses still were in their prime,
45 When like Apollo he came forth to warme
Our eares, or like a Mercury to charme!
Nature her selfe was proud of his designes
And joy'd to weare the dressing of his lines
Which were so richly spun, and woven so fit,
50 As, since, she will vouchsafe no other Wit.
The merry Greeke, tart Aristophanes,
Neat Terence, witty Plautus, now not please;
But antiquated, and deserted lye
As they were not of Natures family.
55 Yet must I not give Nature all: Thy Art,
My gentle Shakespeare, must enjoy a part.
For though the Poets matter, Nature be,
His Art doth give the fashion. And, that he,
Who casts to write a living line, must sweat,
60 (Such as thine are) and strike the second heat
Upon the Muses anvile: turne the same,
(And himselfe with it) that he thinkes to frame;
Or for the lawrell, he may gaine a scorne,
For a good Poet's made, as well as borne.
65 And such wert thou. Looke how the fathers face
Lives in his issue, even so, the race
Of Shakespeares minde, and manners brightly shines
In his well torned, and true-filed lines:
In each of which, he seemes to shake a Lance,
70 As brandish't at the eyes of Ignorance.
Sweet Swan of Avon! what a sight it were
To see thee in our waters yet appeare,

46 *Mercury:* Horace called him "Lord of the curved lyre," an instrument
with which he charmed Apollo, the god of poetry, after he had stolen his
oxen.

50 *As:* that.   54 *As:* as if.   59 *casts:* proposes.

64 *For a good Poets made, as well as borne.* The converse of the Latin
proverb *poeta nascitur non fit.*

68 *torned:* turned.   69 *shake a Lance:* a play upon Shakespeare's name.

71 *Swan of Avon:* The swan is a favourite image for an admired poet.

And make those flights upon the bankes of Thames,
    That so did take Eliza, and our James!
75 But stay, I see thee in the Hemisphere
    Advanc'd, and made a Constellation there!
Shine forth, thou Starre of Poets, and with rage,
    Or influence, chide, or cheere the drooping Stage;
Which, since thy flight from hence, hath mourn'd like night,
80   And despaires day, but for thy Volumes light.

76 *Constellation:* The reference is to the constellation Cygnus.

77-8 *with rage,/Or influence:* "Influence" was originally an astrological term, meaning "emanation from the stars affecting the character of humans". As used by Jonson and Pope (see *Dunciad*, Variorum of 1729, III, 114), the word means "kindly effect", in contradistinction to *rage* or "violent anger".

80 *Volumes:* i.e. volume's

Robert Herrick

THE author of *Hesperides and Noble Numbers* (published 1648) was educated at Westminster School and St. John's College, Cambridge. He was the son of a goldsmith in Cheapside and, on his return to London from the university, became one of the Tribe of Ben who sat at the feet of Jonson in his tavern debates. He then took holy orders and went to live in remote Devon, where he liked the fellowship of his parishioners so little that he was in the habit of drinking with his favourite pig in the garden. J. C. Squire describes him as "a sensualist of the Arcadian type". Rural simplicity of theme subtly hides his meticulous craftsmanship, in which he resembles Horace; but his ingenious rhythms and love of country festivals are characteristically Elizabethan and English. His debt to Jonson and the Latin poets is his happy, but not serious, moralizing. In convivial and amorous mood, he is aptly described as the English Anacreon. The text of the following poem is from the standard Oxford edition of L. C. Martin (1956).

TO HIS HONOURED AND MOST INGENIOUS FRIEND MR. CHARLES COTTON

CHARLES COTTON (1630-87), friend of Izaak Walton and translator of Montaigne's *Essays*, added the dialogue between Piscator and Viator to *The Compleat Angler*, in the fifth edition. At his estate, Beresford Hall, Staffordshire, near the River Dove (one of the best trout-streams in

England), he entertained his friends and wrote witty and graceful poetry.
In *Scarronides* he travestied Vergil; and Charles Lamb thought highly of his
poem "The New Year". Herrick's tribute is another fourteen-lined poem
in epigrammatic couplets.

> For brave comportment, wit without offence,
> Words fully flowing, yet of influence:
> Thou art that man of men, the man alone,
> Worthy the Publique Admiration:
> 5 Who with thine owne eyes read'st what we doe write,
> And giv'st our Numbers Euphonie, and weight.
> Tel'st when a Verse springs high, how understood
> To be, or not borne of the Royall-blood.
> What State above, what Symmetrie below,
> 10 Lines have, or sho'd have, thou the best canst show.
> For which (my Charles) it is my pride to be,
> Not so much knowne, as to be lov'd of thee.
> Long may I live so, and my wreath of Bayes,
> Be lesse anothers Laurell, then thy praise.

8 *of the Royall-blood:* of genuine merit.

13 *wreath of Bayes:* a woven garland of sprigs of the bay-tree or laurel,
used to crown victors or poets.

Sir John Denham

LIKE Herrick, Denham was the son of a London goldsmith, though born in
Dublin. He was a student of Trinity College, Oxford, and Lincoln's Inn,
being intended for the law. His claims to literary fame are based on his
poetic description of the Thames in *Cooper's Hill*, and his blank-verse
melodrama *The Sophy* (1641). T. H. Banks says of Denham that he shares
with Waller the honour of being "the father of the Augustan closed
couplet". The text of the following poem is from Banks's edition of the
Poetical Works (Yale University Press, 1928), the first critical edition since
the publication of the *Poems and Translations* in 1668. Denham was buried
in Westminster Abbey. His slender output contained no love poetry, the
neatly turned couplets being mainly didactic or pious, eulogistic or elegiac.

TO SIR RICHARD FANSHAW, UPON HIS TRANSLATION OF PASTOR FIDO

THIS poem, with its notable observations on the art of verse translation, was probably written in 1643 or 1644, and was published in 1648, Fanshawe (1608–66) was the popular translator of Guarini's *Il Pastor Fido* (*The Faithful Shepherd*), published in the same year. Denham was justly praised for the strength and purity of his diction.

Such is our Pride, our Folly, or our Fate,
That few but such as cannot write, Translate.
But what in them is want of Art, or voice,
In thee is either Modesty or Choice.
5 Whiles this great piece, restor'd by thee doth stand
Free from the blemish of an Artless hand,
Secure of Fame, thou justly dost esteem
Less honour to create; than to redeem.
Nor ought a Genius less than his that writ,
10 Attempt Translation; for transplanted wit,
All the defects of air and soil doth share,
And colder brains like colder Climates are:
In vain they toil, since nothing can beget
A vital spirit, but a vital heat.
15 That servile path thou nobly dost decline
Of tracing word by word, and line by line.
Those are the labour'd births of slavish brains,
Not the effects of Poetry, but pains;
Cheap vulgar arts, whose narrowness affords
20 No flight for thoughts, but poorly sticks at words.
A new and nobler way thou dost pursue
To make Translations and Translators too.
They but preserve the Ashes, thou the Flame,
True to his sense, but truer to his fame.
25 Foording his current, where thou find'st it low
Let'st in thine own to make it rise and flow;
Wisely restoring whatsoever grace
It lost by change of Times, or Tongues, or Place.
30 Nor fetter'd to his Numbers, and his Times,
Betray'st his Musick to unhappy Rimes,

Nor are the nerves of his compacted strength
Stretch'd and dissolv'd into unsinnewed length:
Yet after all, (lest we should think it thine)
Thy spirit to his circle dost confine.

35 New names, new dressings, and the modern cast,
Some Scenes, some persons alter'd, had out-fac'd
The world, it were thy work; for we have known
Some thank't and prais'd for what was less their own.
That Masters hand which to the life can trace

40 The airs, the lines, and features of a face,
May with a free and bolder stroke express
A varyed posture, or a flatt'ring Dress;
He could have made those like, who made the rest,
But that he knew his own design was best.

34 *Thy spirit to his circle:* a reference to the magician's use of the circle as a protective device.

Edmund Waller

EDUCATED at Eton and Cambridge, Waller entered Parliament at sixteen. He was a cousin of Oliver Cromwell and nephew of John Hampden. The Sacharissa to whom he addressed many of the celebrated amatory poems was Lady Dorothy Sidney, who married Lord Spencer in 1639. Though he was mainly a Royalist, Waller's political vacillation and intrigue during the Civil War nearly cost him his life. He was heavily fined and banished to France until the Restoration. His first volume of verse was published in the same year as Milton's, viz. 1645; a fuller and corrected edition appeared in 1664. Typically, he wrote panegyrics on Cromwell and Charles II, and was rallied on the fact that the former was much the better of the two. The most graceful and perfect of his poems is "Go, lovely Rose" (see p. 123). *The Second Part of Mr. Waller's Poems* was published posthumously in 1690, with a preface by Francis Atterbury, whose flattering estimate of the poet needs to be corrected by Edmund Gosse's (*From Shakespeare to Pope*). Atterbury claimed Waller as a refiner of English and creator of the Augustan age, whose style was as mature at twenty as at fourscore years. Gosse thought that Waller narrowed the scope of English verse, and had achieved his prosaic Augustan precision by the year of Shakespeare's First Folio (1623). The texts of the Waller poems in this collection are from Johnson's *Works of the English Poets* (edition 1790), Vol. 16.

TO MY LORD FALKLAND

LUCIUS CARY (1610–43) became the second Viscount Falkland in 1633. Jonson wrote a Pindaric ode (printed in this volume, p. 70) on his friendship with Sir Henry Morison, whose sister, Lettice, Falkland married in 1630. Falkland's father disapproved of the marriage, and the son took military service in Holland; but he returned on his father's death three years later, and lived in retirement at Great Tew. He belonged to a group that advocated latitudinarian reforms in the Anglican church. He was killed at the battle of Newbury in 1643.

Brave Holland leads, and with him Falkland goes.
    Who hears this told, and does not strait suppose
We send the Graces and the Muses forth,
To civilize and to instruct the North?
5 Not that these ornaments make swords less sharp;
Apollo bears as well his bow as harp:
And though he be the patron of that spring,
Where in calm peace the sacred virgins sing;
He courage had to guard th' invaded throne
10 Of Jove, and cast the ambitious Giant down.
    Ah, noble friend! with what impatience all
That know thy worth, and know how prodigal

1 *Brave Holland leads:* Henry Rich, Earl of Holland, was appointed General of Horse in the Bishop's War in February 1639, which dates the poem as probably written in about March of that year. Holland was ignominiously defeated at Kelso on June 3. Falkland applied for command of a troop of horse, and was refused. Consequently he "went as a volunteer with the Earl of Essex", according to Clarendon.

4 *the North:* Scotland. Waller comes near to thinking of England and Scotland as one state, which they were not, in spite of the Stuart succession. At the time of writing of the poem, the war does not seem to have started, or "brave Holland" would have been a misnomer.

7 *the patron of that spring:* Apollo, associated with the nine Muses, virgin daughters of Zeus and Mnemosyne, Goddess of Memory. The Muses dwelt by the fountain Hippocrene (pierced by the hoof of Pegasus) on Mount Helicon, and were the inspirers of poets and musicians. Poetry and music were always associated in Greece.

10 *the ambitious Giant:* Tityus, who insulted Latona, the mother of Apollo and Artemis, and was pierced by their arrows.

Of thy great soul thou art (longing to twist
Bays with that ivy, which so early kiss'd
15   Thy youthful temples) with what horror we
Think on the blind events of war and thee!
To fate exposing that all-knowing breast
Among the throng, as cheaply as the rest:
Where oaks and brambles (if the copse he burn'd)
20   Confounded lie, to the same ashes turn'd.
    Some happy wind over the ocean blow
This tempest yet, which frights our island so!
Guarded with ships, and all the sea our own,
From Heaven this mischief on our heads is thrown.
25   In a late dream, the Genius of this land,
Amaz'd, I saw, like the fair Hebrew stand;
When first she felt the twins begin to jar,
And found her womb the seat of civil war.
Inclin'd to whose relief, and with presage
30   Of better fortune for the present age,
Heaven sends, quoth I, this discord for our good;
To warm, perhaps, but not to waste our blood:

13-15 (*longing to twist/Bays with that ivy . . .*): Ivy was wreathed round the
thyrsus of Bacchus, but was also appropriate to the poet, as in Horace,
Odes, I. i. 29, and Vergil, *Eclogue* VII, 25. In the eighth *Eclogue*, which Vergil
dedicated to Pollio on his return from a campaign against the Parthini in
Illyricum in 39 B.C., lines 11–13 read:

> Accipe iussis
> carmina coeptu tuis atque hanc sine tempora circum
> inter victrices hederam tibi serpere laurus . . .

in which *serpere* means "twist" and *tempora* "temples". Waller suggests
Falkland's desire to mingle the arts of poetry and war.

19 *oaks and brambles:* i.e. in warfare the commanders and soldiers suffer a
common fate.

22 *This tempest:* the coming war with the Scottish Presbyterians.

25 *The Genius of this land:* not necessarily a specific personification like
Britannia. Waller seems to think of England and Scotland as one state,
divided by the prospect of civil war.

26 *the fair Hebrew:* Rebecca, mother of the twins Isaac and Esau.

To raise our drooping spirits, grown the scorn
Of our proud neighbours; who ere long shall mourn
35 (Though now they joy in our expected harms)
We had occasion to resume our arms.
   A lion so with self-provoking smart
(His rebel tail scourging his nobler part)
Calls up his courage; then begins to roar,
40 And charge his foes, who thought him mad before.

34 *our proud neighbours:* England kept out of the wars raging in Europe, and counted for little in European politics.

37 *A lion:* Waller refers to England, temporarily under a cloud. The picture of a lion, working itself up by lashing its tail, is common in mediaeval bestiaries.

38 *his nobler part:* the lion's breast.

TO HIS WORTHY FRIEND MASTER EVELYN, UPON HIS TRANSLATION OF LUCRETIUS

JOHN EVELYN (1620-1706), one of the founders of the Royal Society, went to Balliol College, Oxford, and, though intended for the law, found his niche after the Restoration in the service of the Government. He spent many years abroad in France and Italy during the civil disturbances and was associated with Waller and a group of friends in Paris. He kept a diary of over 700 pages from 1640 till his death; but this valuable record remained in manuscript until 1818. In his long life of unheroic loyalty to the monarchy, horticulture was second only in importance to religion. *Sylva*, his treatise on arboriculture, was responsible for the planting of many thousands of trees in England to replace the consumption of wood in domestic hearths and furnaces. Evelyn translated in 1656 the first of the six books of *De Rerum Natura*, and so influenced the 1685 translation of Dryden. Lucretius (94-55 B.C.) embodied in this difficult poem the simple common-sense philosophy of Epicurus, with its acceptance of determinism and freedom from the apprehension of death. On this he engrafted the theory of the atomic structure of the universe derived from Empedocles, Democritus and Leucippus. He complained of the inadequacies of the business-like Latin vocabulary for his task. His invocation of Venus strongly influenced the secular vision of that goddess in Botticelli's *Primavera*. Waller, like Voltaire, wittily interprets the philosophy of Lucretius as a championship of democratic freedom.

Lucretius (with a stork-like fate,
Born and translated in a state)
Comes to proclaim in English verse,
No monarch rules the universe:
5 But chance and atoms make this All
In order democratical;
Where bodies freely run their course,
Without design, or fate, or force.
And this in such a strain he sings,
10 As if his Muse, with Angels' wings,
Had soar'd beyond our utmost sphere,
And other worlds discover'd there.
For his immortal, boundless wit,
To nature does no bounds permit;
15 But boldly has remov'd those bars
Of heaven, and earth, and seas, and stars,
By which they were before suppos'd,
By narrow wits, to be inclos'd;
Till his free Muse threw down the pale,
20 And did at once dispark them all.

1-2 (*with a stork-like fate, etc.*): Sir Thomas Browne in *Pseudodoxia Epidemica*, Book III, Chapter XXVII, has the following among the vulgar errors concerning animals, "which examined, prove either false or dubious:

§3. That storks are to be found, and will only live, in Republikes or free States, is a petty conceit to advance the opinion of popular policies, and from Antipathies in nature, to disparage Monarchical government. But how far agreeable unto truth, let them consider who read in Pliny, that among the Thessalians who were governed by Kings, and much abounded with Serpents, it was no less than capital to kill a Stork. That the Ancient Egyptians honoured them, whose government was from all times Monarchical." [Professor R. Birley kindly drew my attention to this passage.]

Waller says wittily that Lucretius had the misfortune to be born under a republican commonwealth (one of the seventeenth-century meanings of *State*), and to be translated in England under a similar government.

5-12 Waller gives a brief account of the theme of *De Rerum Natura*. He suggests that a democratic universe, composed of unrelated atoms, would be dependent entirely on chance, which is unthinkable, compared with a universe under the control of God.

So vast this argument did seem,
That the wise author did esteem
The Roman language (which was spread
O'er the whole world, in triumph led)
25   A tongue too narrow to unfold
The wonders which he would have told.
This speaks thy glory, noble friend!
And British language does commend:
For here, Lucretius whole we find,
30   His words, his music, and his mind.
Thy art has to our country brought
All that he writ, and all he thought.
Ovid translated, Virgil too,
Shew'd long since what our tongue could do:
35   Nor Lucan we, nor Horace spar'd;
Only Lucretius was too hard.
Lucretius, like a Fort, did stand
Untouch'd; till your victorious hand
Did from his head this garland bear,
40   Which now upon your own you wear.
A garland! made of such new bays,
And sought in such untrodden ways;
As no man's temples e'er did crown,
Save this great author's, and your own.

UPON HER MAJESTY'S NEW BUILDINGS
AT SOMERSET HOUSE

AFTER the Restoration, Henrietta Maria, Dowager Queen of Charles I,
lived at Somerset House in the Strand, built by John Thynne on the death of
Henry VIII in 1547. The building, named after the Lord Protector, was an
early example of classical architecture in England. Denmark House, as it
was later called, was a present to the Queen, who married Charles in 1625.
The water-gate on the Thames and the garden front had been rebuilt by
Inigo Jones in 1623, and a chapel was added in 1630, when the Queen
(according to Carola Oman) "with her own hands helped to lay the first
square corner-stones". The buildings became dilapidated during the
Commonwealth, and the Queen stayed at Whitehall and Greenwich Palace
after the Restoration. A new gallery, with full-length windows on the
Thames side, after Jones's designs of 1638, was added in 1661, as well as an

Italian garden, paved walks and avenues. The Queen Mother left England for good in 1665, the year Waller's poem was written, and the buildings were demolished by Sir William Chambers in 1778. Once, after dining too well at Somerset House, Waller fell down the full flight of the water-stairs.

> Great Queen! that does our Island bless,
> With Princes and with Palaces:
> Treated so ill, chac'd from your throne,
> Returning, you adorn the town;
> 5 And, with a brave revenge, do show
> Their glory went and came with you.
>
>   While peace from hence, and you, were gone,
> Your houses in that storm o'erthrown,
> Those wounds which civil rage did give,
> 10 At once you pardon and relieve.
>
>   Constant to England in your love,
> As birds are to their wonted grove;
> Though by rude hands their nests are spoil'd,
> There, the next spring, again they build.
>
> 15   Accusing some malignant star,
> Not Britain, for that fatal war;
> Your kindness banishes your fear,
> Resolv'd to fix for ever here.
>
>   But what new Mine this work supplies?
> 20 Can such a pile from ruin rise?
> This like the first creation shows,
> As if at your command it rose.
>
>   Frugality and bounty too,
> (Those diff'ring virtues) meet in you;
> 25 From a confin'd, well-manag'd, store,
> You both employ and feed the poor.
>
>   Let foreign Princes vainly boast
> The rude effects of pride and cost;

2 *Palaces:* probably a reference to Greenwich Palace, built for the Queen by Inigo Jones in 1633.

23-6 *Frugality and bounty too:* The Queen Mother was a careful manager and examined her accounts weekly. But a good part of her income was devoted to feeding the poor and helping defaulters in debtors' prisons.

Of vaster fabrics, to which they
30   Contribute nothing, but the pay.
     This, by the Queen herself design'd,
Gives us a pattern of her mind:
The state and order does proclaim
The genius of that Royal Dame.
35   Each part with just proportion grac'd;
And all to such advantage plac'd;
That the fair view her window yields,
The town, the river, and the fields,
Entering, beneath us we descry;
40   And wonder how we came so high.
     She needs no weary steps ascend;
All seems before her feet to bend:
And here, as she was born, she lies;
High, without taking pains to rise.

2. EPITAPHS

LATIN and Greek were languages well adapted to the epitaph, and the succinct epigram was the ideal style for public inscriptions. Before the seventeenth century English epitaphs, usually in iambic couplets, seldom exceeded fourteen lines. Elegies, such as Carew's "Upon the death of the Deane of St. Pauls" and Milton's "Lycidas" were longer, and in decorous, slow-moving measures. They often contained mythological borrowings and allusions, to test the educated reader's skill in recognition. In short, the elegy was erudite and artistically proportioned, designed for aesthetic appreciation of work accomplished to the honour of a nation. But whether an epitaph or an elegy, the poem must have human and stylistic dignity.

Sir Thomas Wyatt

THE poet was born at Allington Castle on the Medway, and educated at St. John's College, Cambridge. He was in the service of Henry VIII from his thirteenth year, and the King later employed him on missions to Spain, France and Italy. An affair with Anne Boleyn brought him into disfavour, and he was imprisoned in the Tower in 1536 and 1541, but afterwards pardoned. Many of his poems were first published in Tottel's *Songes and*

Sonettes in 1557. He wrote sonnets (after Petrarch), love songs, satires (in the style of Luigi Alamanni), Horatian epistles, and translations of the penitential psalms, becoming the centre and inspirer of a group of "courtly makers", the forerunners of Sidney, Raleigh, Campion and the Cavalier poets. The love-songs are often in the style of the French and Italian complaint, favoured by Chaucer and Serafino, whose poetry he admired. He is a belated mediaevalist, nearer in spirit to Chaucer than to Donne. He is seldom a mere translator, preferring to adapt Italian and French models to the genius of the English tongue. His versatility includes exercises in the classical style, which reveal an ample scholarship. The texts of Wyatt's poems are from Kenneth Muir's collected edition for "The Muses Library", 1949.

AN EPITAPHE OF SIR THOMAS GRAVENER, KNYGHT

THIS poem is signed "W" in the Harleian MS. 78 of the British Museum, which contains only two other of Wyatt's poems. The attribution of this epitaph to Wyatt is doubtful, because the only Thomas Gravener traceable was knighted some years after Wyatt's death. The Gravener referred to in this poem may have been the father of the known man. The tribute is simple in form and language, and a good example of the plain style Wyatt adopted for the Tudor lyric.

> Under this stone ther lyethe at rest
> A frendly man, a worthie knyght,
> Whose hert and mynde was ever prest
> To favor truthe, to farther ryght.
>
> 5 The poores defence, his neighbors ayde,
> Most kynde always unto his kyne,
> That stint all stryf that myght be stayed,
> Whose gentell grace great love dyd wyne.
>
> A man that was full ernest sett
> 10 To serve his prince at all assayes:
> No sycknes cowlde hym from that lett,
> Which was the shortnygne of his dayes.

3 *prest:* impelled. **6** *kyne:* kin.
7 *stint:* stopped. *stryf:* Foxwell (1913) and Tillyard (1929) both have *service;* but the reading of the MS. is *stryf,* which is right for the context.
8 *wyne:* win.

His lyf was good, he dyed full well;
The bodie here, the sowle in blys.
15   With length of wordes whie shoulde I tell,
Or farther shewe that well knowne is.

Sins that the tears of more and lesse
Rightwell declare his worthynes.

Vivit post junera virtus.

17 *Sins:* since.   *more and lesse:* distinguished and less distinguished
persons.

Henry Howard, Earl of Surrey

THOUGH Surrey was in the eighteenth century regarded as a smoother,
more refined and therefore more polished poet than Wyatt, that superiority
is now seen to be no more than a greater regularity of rhythm. Yet there is
substance in Thomas Warton's estimate of him as "the first English classical
poet". He was a brave, even pugnacious, man, who was several times in
trouble for riotous behaviour. He served in several minor wars. Both he and
his son were beheaded for treason. Many of his poems were published in
Tottel's *Miscellany*, and eighteen are in the Arundel Harington MS. of
Tudor poetry. They demonstrate his interest in pastoral and elegiac poetry,
as well as in epigram and epic. He made a rather heavy-footed blank verse
translation of Vergil's *Æneid*, Books II and IV, which is as stiff as the tragedy
Gorboduc. It is possible that Spenser owes something to the purity and
elegance of his syntax, especially in stanza form; he preserves accent more
certainly than Wyatt.

ON SIR THOMAS WYATT

GOOD judges believe this to be the finest of Surrey's poems. It has not only
the generous admiration of a younger for an older poet, but a humanist's
assessment of Wyatt's qualities as a man. There is an epigrammatic con-
cision in the language, too, that gives a much needed firmness to Surrey's
verse. Normally, he is content with a tame correctness, such as poets of a
silver age use. Here he corrects his usual monotony in the disposition of
pauses. H. E. Rollins argues that this was the first of Surrey's poems to appear
in print (written 1542). The text of the poem is taken from *Poems*, ed.
Emrys Jones (Clarendon Press, 1964).

W.   resteth here, that quick could never rest:
   Whose heavenly giftes encreased by disdayn,
And vertue sank the deper in his brest.
Such profit he by envy could obtain.
5   A hed, where wisdom misteries did frame:
   Whose hammers bet styll in that lively brayn,
As on a stithe: where that some work of fame
Was dayly wrought, to turne to Britaines gayn.
   A visage, stern, and myld: where bothe did grow,
10 Vice to contemne, in vertue to rejoyce:
Amid great stormes, whom grace assured so,
To lyve upright, and smile at fortunes choyce.
   A hand, that taught, what might be sayd in ryme:
   That reft Chaucer the glory of his wit:
15 A mark, the which (unparfited, for time)
Some may approche, but never none shall hit.
   A toung, that served in forein realmes his king:
   Whose courteous talke to vertue did enflame
Eche noble hart: a worthy guide to bring
20 Our English youth, by travail, unto fame.
   An eye, whose judgement none affect could blinde,
Frendes to allure, and foes to reconcile:
Whose persing loke did represent a mynde
With vertue fraught, reposed, voyd of gyle.
25 A hart, where drede was never so imprest,
   To hyde the thought, that might the trouth avance:

1 *quick:* alive.

2 *encreased by disdayn:* i.e. "were aroused by his anger" (because of "envy" in line 4).

5 *misteries:* pregnant meanings.

6 *Whose hammers bet:* with the implied image of the mind as a "forge": *bet* is the past tense of *beat*.

11 *grace:* used in the Catholic sense of "heavenly election". This enabled him to smile at the whims of fate (see line 12).

15 *unparfited, for time:* unperfected, because of the shortness of his life.

21 *affect:* partiality.

25-6 Fear did not induce him to conceal his thoughts when truth was at stake.

In neyther fortune loft, nor yet represt,
To swell in wealth, or yeld unto mischance.
   A valiant corps, where force, and beawty met:
30 Happy, alas, to happy, but for foes:
Lived, and ran the race, that nature set:
Of manhodes shape, where she the molde did lose.
   But to the heavens that simple soule is fled:
Which left with such, as covet Christ to know,
35 Witnesse of faith, that never shall be ded:
Sent for our helth, but not received so.
Thus, for our gilte, this jewel have we lost:
The earth his bones, the heavens possesse his gost.

27 *loft:* i.e. aloft, elated or elevated.

29 *corps:* pronounced as, and the original spelling of, *corpse*, which from the fourteenth to eighteenth century could also mean a living person.

30 *to:* i.e. too.

Ben Jonson

EPITAPH ON SALOMON PAVY, A CHILD OF QUEEN ELIZABETH'S CHAPEL

THIS delightful poem is self-explanatory, and classical in its conception of life as a battle-ground of opposed forces, human personalities being the victims.

    Weepe with me all you that read
      This little storie:
    And know, for whom a teare you shed,
      Death's selfe is sorry.
5   'Twas a child, that so did thrive
      In grace, and feature,
    As Heaven and Nature seem'd to strive
      Which own'd the creature.
    Yeeres he numbred scarse thirteene
10   When Fates turn'd cruell,
    Yet three fill'd Zodiackes had he beene
      The stages jewell;

11 *three fill'd Zodiackes:* three years.

And did act (what now we mone)
   Old men so duely,
15 As, sooth, the Parcae thought him one,
   He plai'd so truely.
So, by error, to his fate
   They all consented;
But viewing him since (alas, too late)
20   They have repented.
And have sought (to give new birth)
   In bathes to steepe him;
But, being so much too good for earth,
   Heaven vowes to keepe him.

15 *Parcae:* Fates.
22 *In bathes:* presumably of tears. The imagery is extravagant for Jonson.

Henry King

THE author of "The Exequy", and friend of Ben Jonson, Donne, Izaak Walton and John Hales, was the son of the Bishop of London, one of a long line of clerics. He was educated at Westminster School and Christchurch, Oxford. By 1639 he had risen to be Dean of Rochester. Shortly before the Civil War, he became Bishop of Chichester, but was driven from his palace by the soldiers of Sir William Waller, who had negotiated the surrender of the city. His *Poems* were published in 1657 and 1700, and the text of those selected comes from *The Poems of Henry King*, ed. John Sparrow (Nonesuch Press, 1925). For an amateur poet King had a remarkably musical quality; for he was a great lover of psalmody, and a middle-of-the-way translator of biblical poetry.

AN EPITAPH ON HIS MOST HONOURED FRIEND, RICHARD, EARL OF DORSET

DORSET was the third Earl, and died young in March 1624. The modernity and competence of the style in this tribute show that King, with Waller, Godolphin and others, was a skilful user of the couplet well before Dryden. But it is noteworthy that several of the distiches are not closed ones.

Let no profane ignoble foot tread neer
This hallow'd peece of earth; Dorset lies here.
A small sad relique of a noble spirit,
Free as the air, and ample as his merit;
5   Whose least perfection was large, and great
Enough to make a common man compleat.
A soul refin'd and cull'd from many men,
That reconcil'd the sword unto the pen,
Using both well. No proud forgetting Lord,
10 But mindful of mean names and of his word.
One that did love for honour, not for ends,
And had the noblest way of making friends
By loving first. One that did know the Court,
Yet understood it better by report
15 Then practice, for he nothing took from thence
But the kings favour for his recompence.

One for religion, or his countreys good,
That valu'd not his Fortune nor his blood.
One high in fair opinion, rich in praise;
20 And full of all we could have wisht, but dayes.

He that is warn'd of this, and shall forbear
To vent a sigh for him, or lend a tear;
May he live long and scorn'd, unpiti'd fall,
And want a mourner at his funerall.

Thomas Carew

THE *Poems* of Carew were posthumously published in 1640. There is a large number of manuscripts, with evidence of careful revision; but there are unsolved problems of authorship. Viscount Falkland, in *Ionsonus Virbius*, associated Carew with "that inspired train" that included Digby, Killigrew, Mayne, Godolphin and Waller; but Pope spoke of them contemptuously as "The mob of gentlemen who wrote with ease". He was educated at Merton College, Oxford, and then admitted to the Middle Temple. Tiring of the law, he went to Italy as secretary to the Ambassador, Sir Dudley Carleton; later he accompanied Lord Herbert of Cherbury on a

similar mission to Paris. In 1630 he became a Groom of His Majesty's
Chamber. For the Court, he produced the masque *Coelum Britannicum* in
1633. The poems are the elegant fancies of a cavalier idler, whom Clarendon
described in Jonsonian terms as "a person of pleasant and facetious wit".

AN ELEGIE UPON THE DEATH OF THE DEANE OF PAULS, DR. JOHN DONNE

CAREW admired Jonson, but loved Donne. "The Rapture" and this elegy
are the best known of his writings. The appreciation of Donne is extremely
perceptive, and he had the good sense not to follow Donne into realms
where his talents were unequal. Donne died in 1631; when his *Poems*
appeared two years later, they included elegies by numerous hands, Carew's
being one. The present text is from *The Poems of Thomas Carew*, ed. Rhodes
Dunlap (Clarendon Press, 1949), based on the 1633 edition of Donne, the
version in Carew's *Poems* of 1640 being apparently unrevised and inferior.

> Can we not force from widdowed Poetry,
> Now thou art dead (Great Donne) one Elegie
> To crowne thy Hearse? Why yet dare we not trust
> Though with unkneaded dowe-bak't prose thy dust,
> 5 Such as the uncisor'd Churchman from the flower
> Of fading Rhetorique, short liv'd as his houre,
> Dry as the sand that measures it, should lay
> Upon thy Ashes, on the funerall day?
> Have we no voice, no tune? Did'st thou dispense
> 10 Through all our language, both the words and sense?
> 'Tis a sad truth; The Pulpit may her plaine,
> And sober Christian precepts still retaine,
> Doctrines it may, and wholesome Uses frame,
> Grave Homilies, and Lectures, But the flame
> 15 Of thy brave Soule, (that shot such heat and light,
> As burnt our earth, and made our darknesse bright,

1 *widdowed Poetry:* "widowed" because of Donne's death. From the
opening lines it would appear that Carew's was the first tribute penned.

4 *unkneaded dowe-bak't prose:* The epithet *dow-bak't* occurs in Donne's
'Letter to the Lady Carey and Mrs. Essex Riche'. It means "pedestrian" or
"badly finished" and seems to originate from a dialogue of Sir Thomas
More.

5 *uncisor'd:* unscissored, with uncut hair.

7 *the sand that measure it:* i.e. in the hour-glass.

Committed holy Rapes upon our Will,
Did through the eye the melting heart distill;
And the deepe knowledge of darke truths so teach,
20 As sense might judge, what phansie could not reach;)
Must be desir'd for ever. So the fire,
That fills with spirit and heat the Delphique quire,
Which kindled first by thy Promethean breath,
Glow'd here a while, lies quench't now in thy death;
25 The Muses garden with Pedantique weedes
O'rspred, was purg'd by thee; The lazie seeds
Of servile imitation throwne away;
And fresh invention planted, Thou didst pay
The debts of our penurious bankrupt age;
30 Licentious thefts, that make poëtique rage
A Mimique fury, when our soules must bee
Possest, or with Anacreons Extasie,
Or Pindars, not their owne; The subtle cheat
Of slie Exchanges, and the jugling feat
35 Of two-edg'd words, or whatsoever wrong
By ours was done the Greeke, or Latine tongue,
Thou hast redeem'd, and open'd Us a Mine
Of rich and pregnant phansie, drawne a line
Of masculine expression, which had good
40 Old Orpheus seene, Or all the ancient Brood
Our superstitious fooles admire, and hold
Their lead more precious, then thy burnish't Gold,
Thou hadst beene their Exchequer, and no more
They each in others dust, had rak'd for Ore.

15-20 The long interpolation reflects precisely the effect of Donne on many of his contemporaries.

22 *the Delphique quire:* Pythia, the oracle, attended by five priests at Delphi, delivered her prophecies in hexameter verses.

32-3 *Anacreons Extasie,/Or Pindars, not their owne:* a reference to the ineffectual and insincere imitators of Greek lyric poets. The condemnation of servile poetasters continues to line 44.

34 *slie Exchanges:* probably plagiarisms.

40 *Orpheus:* mythical poet, son of the Muse Calliope; his songs could move trees and rocks, and tame the beasts.

45 Thou shalt yield no precedence, but of time,
   And the blinde fate of language, whose tun'd chime
   More charmes the outward sense; Yet thou maist claime
   From so great disadvantage greater fame,
   Since to the awe of thy imperious wit
50 Our stubborne language bends, made only fit
   With her tough-thick-rib'd hoopes to gird about
   Thy Giant phansie, which had prov'd too stout
   For their soft melting Phrases. As in time
   They had the start, so did they cull the prime
55 Buds of invention many a hundred yeare,
   And left the rifled fields, besides the feare
   To touch their Harvest, yet from those bare lands
   Of what is purely thine, thy only hands
   (And that thy smallest worke) have gleaned more
60 Then all those times, and tongues could reape before;
      But thou art gone, and thy strict lawes will be
   Too hard for Libertines in Poetrie.
   They will repeale the goodly exil'd traine
   Of gods and goddesses, which in thy just raigne
65 Were banish'd nobler Poems, now, with these
   The silenc'd tales o' th' Metamorphoses
   Shall stuffe their lines, and swell the windy Page,
   Till Verse refin'd by thee, in this last Age
   Turne ballad rime, Or those old Idolls bee
70 Ador'd againe, with new apostasie;
      Oh, pardon mee, that breake with untun'd verse
   The reverend silence that attends thy herse,

46-9 *the blinde fate of language, etc.:* Carew seems to refer to the dominance of rhyme in English poetry, because its pleases the ear. This disadvantage Donne overcame by his wit.

50-3 *Our stubborne language, etc.:* English is a tough, unmalleable language to handle in poetry; Donne's muscular conceptions are indigestible for genteel poets.

54-60 The extended horticultural image extols the crop Donne reared from the barren soil, exhausted by his predecessors.

61-70 Carew scorns the "Libertines in Poetry", who borrow from Ovid and ancient mythologies to bolster their invention, or to supply their want of poetic sensibility.   **71** *untun'd verse:* unrhythmical or limping verse.

Whose awfull solemne murmures were to thee
More then these faint lines, A loud Elegie,
75 That did proclaime in a dumbe eloquence
The death of all the Arts, whose influence
Growne feeble, in these panting numbers lies
Gasping short winded Accents, and so dies:
So doth the swiftly turning wheele not stand
80 In th' instant we withdraw the moving hand,
But some small time maintaine a faint weake course
By vertue of the first impulsive force:
And so whil'st I cast on thy funerall pile
Thy crowne of Bayes, Oh, let it crack a while,
85 And spit disdaine, till the devouring flashes
Suck all the moysture up, then turne to ashes.
    I will not draw the envy to engrosse
All thy perfections, or weepe all our losse;
Those are too numerous for an Elegie,
90   And this too great, to be express'd by mee.
Though every pen should share a distinct part,
Yet art thou Theme enough to tyre all Art;
Let others carve the rest, it shall suffice
I on thy Tombe this Epitaph incise.

95 *Here lies a King, that rul'd as hee thought fit*
The universall Monarchy of wit;
Here lie two Flamens, and both those, the best,
Apollo's first, at last, the true Gods Priest.

78 *short winded Accents:* The phrase is borrowed from Shakespeare, *I Henry IV*, I. 1. 3.

84 *crack:* i.e. "crackle" in the flames.

79-82; 83-6 These lines contain admirable metaphysical images.

87-92 *draw the envy to engrosse:* Carew does not wish to catalogue all Donne's perfections, lest envy of his reputation be invited. His qualities are inexhaustible.

96 *The universall Monarchy of wit:* This is the brightest of Carew's inventions, befitting Donne as the leader of the metaphysical school.

97-8 *Flamens:* kindlers of sacrificial fires in the Roman religion. The two represent Donne's contribution to poetry (Apollo) and the Christian faith.

John Milton

It is not often realized that Milton's first volume of poems, containing some in Italian and many in Latin, was published in the same year (1645) as Waller's. The Puritan poet, son of a notary, was a Dissenter un-typical of his austerer brethren, as his earlier poems show; his grandfather was actually a Catholic. "The young lady of Christ's" was thrashed by his tutor at Cambridge, and resented freedom-curtailing authority. His *Comus* was produced at Ludlow in 1634, and received encomiums from that great humanist and letter-writer, Sir Henry Wotton, Provost of Eton, who commended the "Dorique delicacy" of Milton's Songs and Odes, and thought them unparalleled in the English language. His publisher, Humphrey Moseley, hailed him as the successor of Spenser. Milton went blind in 1652, largely as a result of his arduous duties as Cromwell's Latin secretary; his sonnets were his only poetical activities during the Commonwealth. *Paradise Lost* was completed in 1664 and he died ten years later. Chronologically, his life is almost contemporary with Waller's. The texts of the Milton poems are from *The Poetical Works of John Milton*, ed. Helen Darbishire (Clarendon Press, 1955, 1961).

AN EPITAPH ON THE MARCHIONESS OF WINCHESTER

The Marchioness died in childbirth in 1631. Thomas Warton reported that a collection of poems on her was made at Cambridge, and calls Milton's an elegiac ode; but the couplet form qualifies it for the *epitaphs*. It is preserved in Sloane MS. 1446 of the British Museum, which contains several contributions from Oxford poets.

> This rich Marble doth enterr
> The honour'd Wife of Winchester,
> A Vicounts daughter, an Earls heir,
> Besides what her vertues fair
> 5 Added to her noble birth,
> More than she could own from Earth.
> Summers three times eight save one
> She had told, alas too soon,
> After so short time of breath,
> 10 To house with darknes, and with death.
> Yet had the number of her days
> Bin as compleat as was her praise,

Nature and fate had had no strife
In giving limit to her life.
15 Her high birth, and graces sweet,
Quickly found a lover meet;
The Virgin quire for her request
The God that sits at marriage feast;
He at their invoking came
20 But with a scarce-wel-lighted flame;
And in his Garland as he stood,
Ye might discern a Cipress bud.
Once had the early Matrons run
To greet her of a lovely son,
25 And now with second hope she goes,
And calls Lucina to her throws;
But whether by mischance or blame
Atropos for Lucina came;
And with remorseles cruelty,
30 Spoil'd at once both fruit and tree:
The haples Babe before his birth
Had burial, yet not laid in earth,
And the languisht Mothers Womb
Was not long a living Tomb,
35 So have I seen som tender slip
Sav'd with care from Winters nip,
The pride of her carnation train,
Pluck't up by som unheedy swain,
Who onely thought to crop the flowr
40 New shot up from vernall showr;
But the fair blossom hangs the head
Side-ways as on a dying bed,
And those Pearls of dew she wears,
Prove to be presaging tears

18 *The God that sits at marriage feast:* Hymen.

22 *A Cipress bud:* Cypress is a symbol of death, which its presence in Hymen's garland would prognosticate.

26 *Lucina:* the Roman goddess of childbirth.

28 *Atropos:* the Fate that cuts the thread of life with her shears.

37 *carnation:* the Clove-Pink, the original species being flesh-coloured.

45 Which the sad morn had let fall
   On her hast'ning funerall.
   Gentle Lady may thy grave
   Peace and quiet ever have;
   After this thy travail sore
50 Sweet rest sease thee evermore,
   That to give the world encrease,
   Shortned hast thy own lives lease;
   Here, besides the sorrowing
   That thy noble House doth bring,
55 Here be tears of perfet moan
   Weept for thee in Helicon,
   And som Flowers, and som Bays,
   For thy Hears to strew the ways,
   Sent thee from the banks of Came,
60 Devoted to thy vertuous name;
   Whilst thou bright Saint high sit'st in glory,
   Next her much like to thee in story,
   That fair Syrian Shepherdess,
   Who after yeers of barrennes,
65 The highly favour'd Joseph bore
   To him that serv'd for her before,
   And at her next birth, much like thee,
   Through pangs fled to felicity,
   Far within the boosom bright
70 Of blazing Majesty and Light,

49 *travail:* probably used in both senses of "child-birth" and "journey" (cf. *rest* in line 50).

52 *lives lease:* In the genitive singular, as in the plural, the *f* of *life* was voiced to *v*.

55 *moan:* grief.

56 *in Helicon:* i.e. by the Muses.

57-60 These lines support the legend of Warton that a group of Cambridge poets composed elegies.

59 *Came:* the Cam, river which flows through Cambridge.

63 *That fair Syrian Shepherdess:* Rachel, wife of Jacob and mother of Joseph. She died in giving birth to Benjamin.

70 *blazing Majesty and Light:* God.

There with thee, new welcom Saint,
Like fortunes may her soul acquaint,
With thee there clad in radiant sheen,
No Marchioness, but now a Queen.

ON SHAKESPEARE

THIS epitaph was first printed (anonymously) in the Second Folio of
Shakespeare, 1632. In the Shakespeare *Poems* of 1640, the tribute bore the
initials of the poet. In the Milton *Poems* of 1645, the text is closer to the
initialled 1640 version than that of the Folio. The first half of the poem
has a notable classical simplicity of diction; but lines 10 to 16 are syntactic-
ally tortuous; while the last two couplets contain a conceit as far-fetched as
anything in Elizabethan poetry.

What needs my Shakespear for his honour'd Bones,
The labour of an age in piled Stones,
Or that his hallow'd reliques should be hid
Under a Star-ypointing *Pyramid*?
5   Dear son of memory, great heir of Fame,
What need'st thou such weak witnes of thy name?
Thou in our wonder and astonishment
Hast built thy self a live-long Monument.
For whilst to th' shame of slow-endeavouring art,
10   Thy easie numbers flow, and that each heart
Hath from the leaves of thy unvalu'd Book,
Those Delphick lines with deep impression took,
Then thou our fancy of it self bereaving,
Dost make us Marble with too much conceaving;
15   And so Sepulcher'd in such pomp dost lie,
That Kings for such a Tomb would wish to die.

4 *Star-ypointing:* some versions of the Folio of 1632 have *starre-ypointed*.
This reading has been rejected.

11 *unvalu'd:* invaluable.

12 *Those Delphick lines with deep impression took:* This seems to refer to
the oracular sayings of Shakespeare that have made a profound impression
on mankind.

Sidney Godolphin

THIS royalist Cornish poet, Member of Parliament for Helston, and enthusiastic suppoiter of the Earl of Strafford, was educated at Exeter College, Oxford. He was killed in the early stages of the Rebellion in an engagement at Chagford; and was praised for his valour and personal qualities by Clarendon in his *History of the Rebellion*. The poems are preserved in the Malone MS. of the Bodleian Library, and Harleian MS. 6917 of the British Museum; they were not collected until G. Saintsbury's *Caroline Poets* (Vol. II) in 1906. The texts of the following poems is from that modernized edition. Thomas Hobbes, the philosopher, valued his verse for its depth and integrity. Some of the poems are metaphysical; but Godolphin is not to be classified, as he is the product of several strains in Elizabethan poetry.

EPITAPH ON LADY RICH

THIS poem was first published in Gauden's *Funerals made Cordials*, 1658. Godolphin displays the same skill in handling the couplet as he does in his translation of the *Æneid*. The grace of the epigrammatic style is seen to reside in the pure diction and careful modulation of the closed couplet.

> Possest of all that nature could bestow,
> All we can wish to be, or seek to know,
> Equal to all the patterns that our mind
> Can frame of good, beyond the good we find:
> 5 All beauties which have power to bless the sight,
> Mixed with transparent virtue's greater light—
> At once producing love and reverence,
> The admiration of the soul and sense:
> The most discerning thoughts, the calmest breast,
> 10 Most apt to pardon, needing pardon least;
> The largest mind, and which did most extend
> To all the laws of Daughter, Wife, and Friend;
> The most allowed example by what line
> To live, what part to follow, what decline;
> 15 Who best all distant virtues reconciled—
> Strict, cheerful, humble, great, severe, and mild,
> Constantly pious to her latest breath,
> Not more a pattern in her life than death:—
> The Lady Rich lies here: more frequent tears
> 20 Have never honour'd any tomb than hers.

John Cleveland

SAINTSBURY'S selection of Cleveland in *The Caroline Poets*, Vol. III (1921) includes only the authenticated poems. Many others are attributed to Cleveland. A reprint of a fuller edition published in 1677 was made by J. M. Berdan in New York in 1903. Cleveland was born at Loughborough, educated at Christ's College, Cambridge, and elected to a fellowship at St. John's in 1634. Owing to his Royalist sympathies, he transferred to Oxford in 1642, but remained in England during the Commonwealth. He was charged before the Council of State by Norwich informers, who resented his biting wit, and sent to prison in Yarmouth for three months. He died as the result of this imprisonment. He was undoubtedly an able man and an intellectual. As a metaphysical poet, he carried the excesses of the school to unfortunate limits, which Dr. Johnson castigated in his essay on Cowley. The many editions of his work in the seventeenth century substantiate his popularity and rivalry with the author of *Hudibras*. Butler and Dryden were both much indebted to him in their satires. He used the octosyllabic couplet with great verve, without being a serious artist. Too much of his poetry is carelessly written and unrevised.

EPITAPH ON THE EARL OF STRAFFORD

THOMAS WENTWORTH, afterwards Earl of Strafford (1593-1641) was educated at St. John's College, Cambridge, and the Inner Temple. He represented Yorkshire in the Parliament of 1621, and four years later, though a Royalist, resisted Charles I's levies for a war with Spain. In 1632 he became Lord Deputy of Ireland, where his administration was high-handed. The King then brought him back to England as his chief adviser. He was impeached by the Long Parliament in 1641, largely owing to his advocacy of the unsuccessful war with Scotland, and executed on Tower Hill. The text of this poem is from Saintsbury's *Caroline Poets*.

> Here lies wise and valiant dust
> Huddled up 'twixt fit and just;
> Strafford, who was hurried hence
> 'Twixt treason and convenience.
> 5   He spent his time here in a mist;
> A Papist, yet a Calvinist;
> His Prince's nearest joy and grief
> He had, yet wanted all relief;

The prop and ruin of the State;
10 The People's violent love and hate;
One in extremes loved and abhorred.
Riddles lie here, or in a word,
Here lies blood; and let it lie
Speechless still and never cry.

AN ELEGY ON BEN JONSON

THIS poem, though not disputed as Cleveland's by most editors, is not included in editions of his poems in 1653 and 1677. It appears, signed, in *Jonsonus Virbius*, 1638.

Who first reformed our stage with justest laws,
And was the first best judge in his own cause;
Who, when his actors trembled for applause,

Could (with a noble confidence) prefer
5   His own, by right, to a whole theatre;
From principles which he knew could not err:

Who to his fable did his persons fit,
With all the properties of art and wit,
And above all that could be acted, writ:

10 Who public follies did to covert drive,
Which he again could cunningly retrive,
Leaving them no ground to rest on and thrive:

Here JONSON lies, whom, had I named before,
In that one word alone I had paid more
15 Than can be now, when plenty makes me poor.

3-6 Probably a reference to Jonson's "Ode to Himself" on the poor reception of his play *The New Inn.*
7 *fable:* plot.
15 *when plenty makes me poor:* This may refer to the numerous other encomiums in *Jonsonus Virbius*, or to the many things the poet feels he might have said, did not his talent fall short of a worthy tribute.

3. EPISTLES

THE number of verse epistles among the poems of Jonson, Donne, Carew, Waller and others, is evidence of the popularity of this genre initiated by Horace, "the enthusiast of moderation", as well as satirist. It is notable that Horace, the father of graceful colloquial ease in writing, penned the *Epistles* soon after the *Sermones*. His Epistles are mainly talks upon moral conduct, and are sometimes regarded as the most polished and mature of his writings. Jonson and the English classicists found the epistle apt for personal philosophy and observations upon men and manners; for correspondence of a civilized social kind which the Latin Augustans called *urbanitas*. Sir Henry Wotton and Joseph Addison are among the best exemplars of this quality in the seventeenth and eighteenth centuries.

Ben Jonson

TO MY LADY COVELL

THE lady is unidentified. Lines 7-12 are a candid self-portrait of the poet in his grossness. The first two couplets exemplify the Horatian wit of gallantry, of which Jonson was a master.

You won not Verses, Madam, you won mee,
    When you would play so nobly, and so free.
A booke to a few lynes: but, it was fit
    You won them too, your oddes did merit it.
5 So have you gain'd a Servant and a Muse:
    The first of which, I feare, you will refuse;
And you may justly, being a tardie, cold,
    Unprofitable Chattell, fat and old,
Laden with Bellie, and doth hardly approach
10 His friends, but to breake Chaires, or cracke a Coach.
His weight is twenty Stone within two pound;
    And that's made up as doth the purse abound.
Marrie the Muse is one, can tread the Aire,
    And stroke the water, nimble, chast, and faire,
15 Sleepe in a Virgins bosome without feare,
    Run all the Rounds in a soft Ladyes eare,

12 *made up:* increased.

Widow or Wife, without the jealousie
    Of either Suitor, or a Servant by.
Such, (if her manners like you) I doe send:
20   And can for other Graces her commend,
To make you merry on the Dressing stoole,
    A mornings, and at afternoones, to foole
Away ill company, and helpe in rime
    Your Joane to passe her melancholie time.
25   By this, although you fancie not the man,
    Accept his Muse; and tell, I know you can,
How many verses, Madam, are your Due!
    I can lose none in tendring these to you.
I gaine, in having leave to keepe my Day,
30   And should grow rich, had I much more to pay.

22 *A mornings, and at afternoons: A* is the abbreviated form of *at* or *on* before consonants.

29 *Day:* fixed date of payment, cf. *Merchant of Venice*, I. 3. 159.

30 Note the paradox in the compliment.

TO THE RIGHT HONOURABLE, THE LORD HIGH TREASURER OF ENGLAND, AN EPISTLE MENDICANT (1631)

THIS letter is addressed, in the extremity of Jonson's old age, to Richard, Lord Weston (1577-1635), Chancellor of the Exchequer and Lord High Treasurer from 1628. He became an unpopular figure, as the differences between Charles I and Parliament over financial matters became acute, Parliament being dissolved in 1629. In another epistle, dated February 17, 1632, when Weston became Earl of Portland, Jonson called him the "Eye of State/Who seldom sleepes! whom bad men only hate". A stroke had left Jonson partially paralysed in 1628, but he lived for nine years in poverty, relieved by a pension from the King. Jonson's petition in rhymed triplets is witty and dignified, not obsequious.

My Lord;
Poore wretched states, prest by extremities,
Are faine to seeke for succours, and supplies
Of Princes aides, or good mens Charities.

Disease, the Enemie, and his Ingineeres,
5   Want, with the rest of his conceal'd compeeres,
Have cast a trench about mee, now, five yeares;

And made those strong approaches, by False braies,
Reduicts, Halfe-moones, Horne-workes, and such close wayes,
The Muse not peepes out, one of hundred dayes;

10   But lyes block'd up, and straightned, narrow'd in,
Fix'd to the bed, and boords, unlike to win
Health, or scarce breath, as she had never bin,

Unlesse some saving-Honour of the Crowne,
Dare thinke it, to relieve, no lesse renowne,
15   A Bed-rid Wit, then a besieged Towne.

4 *Ingineeres:* co-workers.

4-8 The sustained image of warfare in these lines is explained in "a besieged Towne" of line 15, to which Jonson compares himself.

7 *False braies:* protective walls erected before the garrisoned rampart. The French word is *faussebraies.*

8 *Reduicts:* positions in the main rampart, for use when the outer defences (just referred to) have been captured.   *Halfe-moones:* semicircular earthworks to defend a strategic position.   *Horne-workes:* wedge-shaped earthworks to protect positions outside the defences of a besieged town.   *Close wayes:* secret lines of communication.

13 *saving-Honour of the Crowne:* sinecure, or paid post without any duties attached to it.

MARTIAL, BOOK X, EPISTLE 47—VITAM QUAE FACIUNT BEATIOREM

THIS popular epigram of Martial was translated by many poets, including Cowley, whose version has not the freedom, vigour and concision of Jonson's. The spirit and philosophy of Horace pervade the latter; it was he who made this kind of *humanitas* possible. Jonson, anticipating Pope, breaks the regularity of the couplets with a triple rhyme in lines 9 to 11.

The Things that make the happier life, are these,
Most pleasant Martial; Substance got with ease,
Not labour'd for, but left thee by thy Sire;
A Soyle, not barren; a continewall fire;

  5 Never at Law; seldome in office gown'd;
      A quiet mind; free powers; and body sound;
      A wise simplicity; freindes alike-stated;
      Thy table without art, and easy-rated:
      Thy night not dronken, but from cares layd wast;
10 No sowre, or sollen bed-mate, yet a Chast;
      Sleepe, that will make the darkest howres swift-pac't;
      Will to bee, what thou art; and nothing more:
      Nor feare thy latest day, nor wish therfore.

7 *Alike-stated:* in the same circumstances.
8 *Thy table without art, and easy-rated:* hospitality that is unostentatious and accessible.
9 *layd wast:* exempt.
13 *thy latest day:* last day.

Edmund Waller

TO MR. KILLEGREW. UPON HIS ALTERING HIS PLAY *PANDORA*, FROM A TRAGEDY INTO A COMEDY, BECAUSE NOT APPROVED ON THE STAGE

THE staunch Royalist, Sir William Killigrew (1605-93), Governor of Pendennis Castle, Gentleman-Usher to Charles I and Vice-Chamberlain to the Queen Consort, published three plays in 1665, of which *Pandora* was one. Waller's letter was included in the edition.

      Sir, you should rather teach our age the way
      Of judging well, than thus have chang'd your Play:
      You had oblig'd us by employing wit,
      Not to reform Pandora, but the Pit,
  5 For, as the nightingale, without the throng
      Of other birds, alone attends her song:
      While the loud daw, his throat displaying, draws
      The whole assembly of his fellow daws:

So must the writer, whose productions should
10 Take with the vulgar, be of vulgar mould:
Whilst nobler fancies make a flight too high
For common view, and lessen as they fly.

5-12 The extended simile (of the nightingale and the daw) is typical of
Waller, even in short poems.

12 *lessen:* decrease in size.

4. SATIRES AND EXPOSTULATIONS

SATIRE can be either social or personal; both kinds are represented here.
Expostulations are private exasperations, and may be directed against
persons, groups, social types, institutions, or even literary practices, for
instance Jonson's tongue-in-cheek attack on the use of rhyme in poetry. The
models for English classical verse were the Latin poets Catullus, Horace,
Martial and Juvenal. The epigram in the closed couplet proved the most
suitable medium in English for the expression of personal feeling. Horace
wrote his satires (which are really didactic poems) in hexameters, and both
he and his predecessor Lucilius used popular speech for their "Musa
pedestris". If satire is to be ingenious, pointed and witty, economy is
essential.

Sir Walter Raleigh

RALEIGH (the commonest spelling of the name is Ralegh) was a Devonshire
gentleman educated at Oriel College, Oxford. He became a soldier and
seaman, fighting in Ireland, France and the Spanish dominions; a courtier,
a colonizer, who had estates in Ireland and founded a colony in Virginia, a
Member of Parliament, a poet and an historian. At the age of thirty he
caught the notice of the Queen, and his personality dominated the Court
for the next decade; but his pride and ambition made enemies. Disfavour
came with his enforced marriage to Elizabeth Throckmorton, one of the
Queen's maids-of-honour. When restored to the Queen's favour, he was
made Governor of Jersey. Soon after the accession of James I he was falsely
charged as a negotiator with Spain, but defended himself with such courage
and nobility that condemnation turned him into a popular martyr. When
his more favoured associates were pardoned, he was re-committed to the
Tower and there wrote his *History of the World.* In 1617 he was allowed to fit
out an expedition to Guiana that the King might be provided with much

needed gold. The quest for the mine was a failure, and Raleigh lost his son
in a skirmish with Spaniards. When he returned he was basely beheaded on
the sentence of 1603. He was generally thought to have been sacrificed
to appease Spain. He published nothing during his lifetime. Many of his
poems have not survived, and some that have are of dubious authenticity.
Only fragments remain of his long poem *Cynthia* addressed to Queen
Elizabeth. His poetry is personal and passionate, thoughtful and moralizing,
as befitted a courtier, but one who was different from the derivative
fashions. His influence on his contemporaries, even Spenser, was consider-
able. He was not a rebel against conventional Petrarchism, so much as an
individualist. In everything he did he wanted to be different from other
men.

THE LIE

THE gnomic verse of this poem is in the style of the Complaint of the
Middle Ages. In spite of the wrongs and sufferings of his life, Raleigh
is not usually an embittered writer; he held to the Elizabethan fatalist's
axiom "Fortune my Foe". He is grave and proportioned, with little of the
romance one might have expected from the adventurous nature of his life.
Roman stoicism is combined with classical partiality for moralizing reticence
and avoidance of excess. In snatches of translation from the Latin poets in his
History of the World, Raleigh displays admirable restraint and Augustan
manners. He is an early English master of the epigram, and, like Jonson,
finds his favourite rhythms in the couplet and the quatrain. He preserves the
latter from monotony by interspersing multiple rhymes. Perhaps the most
cynical of Raleigh's poems, "The Lie" was published anonymously in
Davison's *Poetical Rapsodie* (1608). The text reproduced here is from Agnes
Latham's edition of the *Poems* for the "Muses Library", 1951.

> Goe soule the bodies guest
>   upon a thankelesse arrant,
> Feare not to touch the best
>   the truth shall be thy warrant:
> 5   Goe since I needs must die,
>   and give the world the lie.

2 *arrant:* a common form of "errand" in Elizabethan literature.

5 *since I needs must die:* This line does not signify that the poem was
written immediately before Raleigh's condemnation to death in 1603;
it was probably composed ten years earlier.

Say to the Court it glowes,
   and shines like rotten wood,
Say to the Church it showes
10   whats good, and doth no good.
If Church and Court reply,
   then give them both the lie.

Tell Potentates they live
   acting by others action,
15 Not loved unlesse they give,
   not strong but by affection.
If Potentates reply,
   give Potentates the lie.

Tell men of high condition,
20   that mannage the estate,
Their purpose is ambition,
   their practise onely hate:
And if they once reply,
   then give them all the lie.

25 Tell them that brave it most,
   they beg for more by spending,
Who in their greatest cost
   seek nothing but commending.
And if they make replie,
30   then give them all the lie.

Tell zeale it wants devotion
   tell love it is but lust
Tell time it meets but motion,
   tell flesh it is but dust.
35 And wish them not replie
   for thou must give the lie.

9-12 Raleigh was a sceptic.
20 *estate:* this was the original form of "state"—a body politic.
25 *brave it most:* swagger most ostentatiously.
33 *meets:* measures.

Tell age it daily wasteth,
   tell honour how it alters.
Tell beauty how she blasteth
40   tell favour how it falters
And as they shall reply,
   give every one the lie.

Tell wit how much it wrangles
   in tickle points of nycenesse,
45 Tell wisedome she entangles
   her selfe in over wisenesse.
And when they doe reply
   straight give them both the lie.

Tell Phisicke of her boldnes,
50   tell skill it is prevention:
Tell charity of coldnes,
   tell law it is contention,
And as they doe reply
   so give them still the lie.

55 Tell fortune of her blindnesse,
   tell nature of decay,
Tell friendship of unkindnesse,
   tell justice of delay.
And if they will reply,
60   then give them all the lie.

Tell Arts they have no soundnesse,
   but vary by esteeming,
Tell schooles they want profoundnes
   and stand too much on seeming.
65 If Arts and schooles reply,
   give arts and schooles the lie.

39 *blasteth:* withers.
44 *in tickle points of nycenesse:* minutiae, trivialities.
50 *skill:* mental ability, sagacity, wit.   *prevention:* frustration.

Tell faith its fled the Citie,
   tell how the country erreth,
Tell manhood shakes off pittie,
70   tell vertue least preferreth
And if they doe reply,
   spare not to give the lie.

So when thou hast as I,
   commanded thee, done blabbing,
75 Although to give the lie,
   deserves no lesse then stabbing,
Stab at thee he that will,
   no stab thy soule can kill.

69-70 The syntax of these two lines is elliptical.

Sir John Davies

THE poet was born near Tisbury, Wiltshire, and educated at Queen's College, Oxford, and the Middle Temple, being called to the Bar in 1595. He wrote Latin epigrams, which gained for him the reputation of "the English Martial", and published two long poems, one on dancing, *Orchestra* (1596), the other, his greatest, *Nosce Teipsum* (1599), on the immortality of the soul, which ran through three editions in the next nine years. He represented Dorsetshire in Parliament in 1601, became Solicitor-General in Ireland two years later, was knighted in 1607, became a judge in 1620, and Lord Chief Justice in 1626, the year of his death. In the seventeenth century Davies was regarded as supreme in English philosophical poetry, the successor of Marcus Aurelius Antoninus.

OF A GULL

THIS satirical portrait belongs to the *Epigrams* probably published in 1597. The text is from A. B. Grosart's edition of the *Poems*, 1869, and is based on the copy in the Malone collection, Bodleian Library, Oxford.

Oft in my laughing rimes, I name a Gull:
But this new terme will many questions breed;
Therefore at first I will expresse at full,
Who is a true and perfect Gull indeed:

1 *Gull:* i.e. an empty-headed fop, easily taken in—hence "gullible".

5 A Gull is he who feares a velvet gowne,
    And, when a wench is brave, dares not speak to her;
    A Gull is he which traverseth the towne,
    And is for marriage known a common woer;
    A Gull is he which while he proudly weares,
10 A silver-hilted rapier by his side;
    Indures the lyes and knocks about the eares,
    Whilst in his sheath his sleeping sword doth bide;
    A Gull is he which weares good handsome cloaths,
    And stands, in Presence, stroaking up his haire,
15 And fills up his unperfect speech with oaths,
    But speaks not one wise word throughout the yeare:
    But to define a Gull in termes precise,—
    A Gull is he which seemes, and is not wise.

6 *brave:* richly dressed.

Ben Jonson

ON POET-APE

THE butt of this diatribe is unknown; but the attack is on a playwright who is also a plagiarist, of whom there were many in Jonson's time. The poem was published in the Jonson Folio of 1616, but was probably written many years earlier. It has been suggested that Shakespeare may be the victim, because of the words "would be thought our chiefe" in the first line.

    Poore Poet-Ape, that would be thought our chiefe,
      Whose workes are eene the fripperie of wit,
    From brocage is become so bold a thiefe,
      As we, the rob'd, leave rage, and pittie it.
5 At first he made low shifts, would picke and gleane,
      Buy the reversion of old playes; now growne
    To'a little wealth, and credit in the scene,
      He takes up all, makes each mans wit his owne.

2 *fripperie:* out-of-date clothes.
3 *brocage:* trade in cast-off wares.
6 *reversion:* rights.

And, told of this, he slights it. Tut, such crimes
10   The sluggish gaping auditor devoures;
He markes not whose 'twas first: and after-times
May judge it to be his, as well as ours.
Foole, as if halfe eyes will not know a fleece
From locks of wooll, or shreds from the whole peece?

A FIT OF RIME AGAINST RIME

THIS is a witty, punning and original poem in falling rhythm. Here, in
embyro, is the metrical ingenuity and pleasantry of Cleveland, Butler and
Swift. In the last twelve lines, Jonson inveighs not only against the tyranny
of rhyme, but against the effects of it on the structure of the verse line.
Jonson and Donne were the major innovators after 1600 in reforming the
syntax and diction of English poetry. They saw that while the distribution
of the pauses determines the rhythm of verse, it is more natural to have the
caesuras coincide with syntactic pauses. Their innovation in diction was the
adaptation of colloquial English to the style and themes of Horace's satires
and epistles. They took the modulation of the line a step farther than
Chaucer, Marlowe and Shakespeare.

Rime, the rack of finest wits,
That expresseth but by fits,
                    True Conceipt,
Spoyling Senses of their Treasure,
5   Cosening Judgement with a measure,
                    But false weight.
Wresting words, from their true calling;
Propping Verse, for feare of falling
                    To the ground.
10   Joynting Syllabes, drowning Letters,
Fastning Vowells, as with fetters
                    They were bound!

2 *by fits:* fitfully, spasmodically.
5 *Cosening:* deceiving.   *measure:* rhythm and metre.
10 *Joynting Syllabes, drowning Letters:* adding syllables, suppressing (or
eliding) letters.
11 *Fastning Vowells:* fixing the quality of vowels.

C

Soone as lazie thou wert knowne,
All good Poëtrie hence was flowne,
15   And Art banish'd.
For a thousand yeares together,
All Pernassus Greene did wither,
And wit vanish'd.
Pegasus did flie away,
20 At the Well no Muse did stay,
But bewailed
So to see the Fountaine drie,
And Apollo's Musique die,
All light failed!
25 Starveling rimes did fill the Stage,
Not a Poët in an Age,
Worth a crowning.
Not a worke deserving Baies,
Nor a lyne deserving praise,
30   Pallas frowning.
Greeke was free from Rimes infection,
Happy Greeke, by this protection,
Was not spoyled.
Whilst the Latin, Queene of Tongues,
35 Is not yet free from Rimes wrongs,
But rests foiled.
Scarce the Hill againe doth flourish,
Scarce the world a Wit doth nourish,
To restore

14 *All good Poetrie:* Jonson refers to the work of classical poets, who did not employ rhyme.

17 *Pernassus:* Parnassus, mountain home of the Muses and Apollo (in the possessive case), governing "Greene".

19-20 *Pegasus:* legendary winged horse, whose hoof, when he took flight from Mount Helicon, struck the earth and created the fountain Hippocrene ("the Well" of line 20).

28 *Baies:* laurel wreath.

30 *Pallas:* Pallas Athene, goddess of wisdom—the Roman Minerva.

35 The bondage of rhyme here refers to its use in mediaeval Latin poetry, especially church hymns.

37 *the Hill:* Parnassus.

40 Phoebus to his Crowne againe;
    And the Muses to their braine;
                    As before.
    Vulgar Languages that want
    Words, and sweetnesse, and be scant
45   Of true measure,
    Tyran Rime hath so abused,
    That they long since have refused
                    Other ceasure.
    He that first invented thee,
50 May his joynts tormented bee,
                    Cramp'd for ever;
    Still may Syllabes jarre with time,
    Stil may reason warre with rime,
                    Resting never.
55 May his Sense, when it would meet
    The cold tumor in his feet,
                    Grow unsounder.
    And his Title be long foole,
    That in rearing such a Schoole,
60   Was the founder.

43 *Vulgar Languages:* the rising vernacular languages and literatures of western Europe.

45 *true measure:* quantitative, not accentual metres.

46 *Tyran:* the original form of *tyrant.*

48 *Other ceasure:* Caesuras are pauses within the line; but rhyme induces end-pauses, and so inhibits caesural variation.

56 *feet:* There is a pun on the divisions of scansion.

Robert Herrick

TO DEAN-BOURN, A RUDE RIVER IN DEVON, BY WHICH SOMETIMES HE LIVED

HERRICK was ordained in 1623, and is thought to have resided in London for the next six years, until he obtained the living of Dean-Prior in Devonshire. As early as 1625 he had earned a reputation as a poet and as the friend of Jonson, Selden and Henry Lawes, who composed music for some of his

lyrics. This poem, which appeared in *Hesperides* (1648), is unlikely to con-
tain his considered views of his parishioners; for Wood in his *Athenae
Oxonienses* (1691-2) reported that he was "much beloved by the gentry
in those parts for his florid and witty Discourse". But solitude in the
country undoubtedly chafed him after his convivial, literary associations
in London. His sister-in-law, who kept house for him, died and was buried
at Dean-Prior in 1643. The quiet, rural life inspired some of his best
poetry. In 1647 Herrick was ejected from his vicarage, as a Royalist,
and lived on charity in the parish of St. Annes, Westminster, London,
until the Restoration. He then returned to Dean-Prior for fourteen years,
and died there.

> Dean-Bourn, farewell; I never look to see
> Deane, or thy warty incivility.
> Thy rockie bottome, that doth teare thy streams,
> And makes them frantick, ev'n to all extreames;
> 5   To my content, I never sho'd behold,
> Were thy streames silver, or thy rocks all gold.
> Rockie thou art; and rockie we discover
> Thy men; and rockie are thy wayes all over.
> O men, O manners; Now, and ever knowne
> 10 To be A Rockie Generation!
> A people currish; churlish as the seas;
> And rude (almost) as rudest Salvages.
> With whom I did, and may re-sojourne when
> Rockes turn to Rivers, Rivers turn to Men.

9 *O men, O manners:* cf. Latin *O tempora, O mores!*

12 *Salvages:* the original form of *savages.*

13-14 The last couplet suggests that the poem may have been written
just after his enforced departure from Dean-Prior in 1647.

LYRICS

GILBERT MURRAY (in *The Classical Tradition in Poetry*) says that lyrical
verse possesses "the quality of metrical construction or architecture"; and
he defines a *lyric* as "the arrangement of a complex form in such a way that
no part stands alone, but each contributes to the value of other parts and to
the main effect of the whole". This account is satisfactory for classical verse,

where the emphasis is on form. Romantic poetry lays it rather on fine thoughts crystallized round an emotion. But whether classic or romantic, the lyric calls for artistic unity and a song-like quality.

The Greek lyrics were clear in vision, and well proportioned in metre and phrasing. Pindar, the creator of the stately moving ode, composed the music as well as the complex metre and the words. Two simpler measures, sapphics and alcaics, were named after the poets who practised and possibly invented them. Their lyrics dealt with personal experiences and feelings; the elegy, a graver poetry in hexameters, offered impersonal and sententious reflections. Both tended to idealization, as in Greek sculpture. The restraint of emotion by reason was an ethic with the Greeks that they communicated to the Romans.

The debt of French and English lyrical verse to the ancients was in theme, attitude, mythological imagery and formal compactness, not metre. It is true that the French tied themselves strictly to the number and value of syllables; but the English lyrists were accentualists, not syllable-counters. Campion describes his poems as "ear-pleasing rhymes, without art". The keynote of the English lyric thus became its spontaneity. In this respect it is nearer in spirit to the shorter poems of Catullus.

5. ODES

IN *The Classical Tradition*, Gilbert Highet defines the ode as "a poem combining personal emotion with deep meditation on a subject of wide scope or broad public interest" (p. 239).

Not only has the ode, in its long history, expressed varied moods, but it has undergone diverse metrical experiments, since Pindar practised it in the fifth century B.C. Literatures of western Europe revived the ode in the sixteenth and seventeenth centuries to give tighter form to the complex and shapeless *Canzone* of the Italian Renaissance, a better example of which is Spenser's *Epithalamion* (1594). The Renaissance itself had preserved the name "ode" for the choral songs of Greek drama. Greek odes like Pindar's were addressed to specific audiences in priestlike tones, sublime and prophetic. The Dorian ode was thus a public utterance, while the Anacreontic secular song was a private one, of a lone singer with his musical instrument.

Pindar wrote in his sixth Olympian ode: "The forehead of every work begun must shine from afar." Hence the dazzling invocations with which the Pindaric odes began. Then came an explanation of the ceremonial occasion, followed by appropriate mythology. Finally, the poet added his moral reflections, or a prayer for the hero celebrated, often the victor at an Olympic Festival. With Pindar, the images were palpable and visual, limited in range to the heroic, prosperous and divine.

The odes of Horace appeal more to modern tastes, because their theme is the piety of temperance and self-discipline in a chaotic and disintegrating world. His odes contain points of rest for the civilized, common-sense precepts that strike home because he finds the inevitable words and the best order. Here one sees, for the first time, humour and verbal irony, poetry with a social and mildly critical tone. Images, though often mythological in origin, have a formal and didactic purpose; Horace is the inventor of the memorable aphoristic phrase. Where the long-winded Pindar used complex stanza forms, Horace preferred simple quatrains; his odes were usually short. Economy of word and objective impartiality were enlivened with a keen wit.

When the ode cultivated by the Pléiade in France came to Britain in the late sixteenth century, it was in the spirit and form of one or other of the great masters of antiquity, usually Pindar. John Southern in his *Pandora* (1584) published translations of some odes of Ronsard, which were loosely Pindaric in structure, but lacking in the Greek poet's Doric nobility and vehemence. Drayton in his *Poems Lyrick and Pastorall* (1606), like Barnabe Barnes before him, called some of his songs odes; but, except when imitating Horace, as in "An Ode written in the Peake" and "To the Virginian Voyage", his odes are transitional and indistinguishable in spirit from the lyrics composed by the Celtic harpists of the middle ages.

Ben Jonson

TO THE IMMORTALL MEMORIE, AND FRIENDSHIP OF THAT NOBLE PAIRE, SIR LUCIUS CARY, AND SIR H. MORISON

THIS poem is described by Carol Maddison in *Apollo and the Nine* as "a superb example of Jonson's Palladian neo-classicism". Jonson had experimented with Pindaric metrical irregularities of line in his "Ode to Sir William Sydney on his Birthday". In the Lucius Cary poem, written in 1629, he preserves the triadic form of strophe, antistrophe and epode, which he calls "Turne", "Counter-Turne" and "Stand", merely translating the Italian Minturno's "volta", "rivolta" and "stanza". The origin of these turns is to be found in the Greek dramatic chorus, which, in its stately movements, divided and reunited for parts of the choral song. Strophe and immediately following antistrophe correspond strictly in syllabic and linear structure. Epode is matched with epode, a briefer and quieter figure, in every third stanza. The whole is a symphonic poem in which the rhythmical units are musical phrases. The only odes of Pindar that survived are the epinician or victory-odes. He was acknowledged throughout the Mediterranean world as the supreme lyric poet of ancient Greece. Few poets in any language have managed his daring images and splendid colouring. The sublimity was beyond the scope of Jonson, who substituted Horace's leisurely pensiveness for Pindar's vehemence. By varying the length of lines in rhymed couplets Jonson captured the visual effect of Pindar without his spirit. Jonson's aim is to comfort Lucius Cary (Viscount Falkland) for the loss of his friend, by telling him that their friendship has become immortal. Henry Morison (1608-29) was the nephew of the Elizabethan traveller, Fynes Morison; Falkland married his sister.

The Turne

Brave Infant of Saguntum, cleare
Thy comming forth in that great yeare,
When the Prodigious Hannibal did crowne
His rage, with razing your immortall Towne.
5   Thou, looking then about,
E're thou wert halfe got out,
Wise child, did'st hastily returne,
And mad'st thy Mothers wombe thine urne.
How summ'd a circle didst thou leave man-kind
10 Of deepest lore, could we the Center find!

The Counter-turne

Did wiser Nature draw thee back,
From out the horrour of that sack?
Where shame, faith, honour, and regard of right
Lay trampled on; the deeds of death, and night,
15 Urg'd, hurried forth, and horld
Upon th'affrighted world:
Sword, fire, and famine, with fell fury met;
And all on utmost ruine set;

1 *Brave Infant of Saguntum:* The prodigy of the new-born child who returned to the womb to die, and so missed the terrors of Hannibal's destruction of Saguntum, at the outset of the Second Punic War in 219 B.C., is described in Livy's *History*.

7 *Wise child:* Pliny records, in his *Natural History*, VII. 3, that it was divine insight that caused the child to avoid birth and so escape the miseries of the world.

9 *How summ'd a circle:* how perfect an example.

10 *lore:* learning.   *Center:* the controlling principle, the key to the mystery.

15 *horld:* hurled. The spelling makes a visual rhyme with *world*.

As, could they but lifes miseries fore-see,
20 No doubt all Infants would returne like thee.

The Stand

For, what is life, if measur'd by the space,
Not by the act?
Or masked man, if valu'd by his face,
Above his fact?
25 Here's one out-liv'd his Peeres,
And told forth fourscore yeares;
He vexed time, and busied the whole State;
Troubled both foes, and friends;
But ever to no ends:
30 What did this Stirrer, but die late?
How well at twentie had he falne, or stood!
For three of his foure-score, he did no good.

The Turne

Hee entred well, by vertuous parts,
Got up and thriv'd with honest arts:
35 He purchas'd friends, and fame, and honours then,
And had his noble name advanc'd with men:
But weary of that flight,
He stoop'd in all mens sight
To sordid flatteries, acts of strife,
40 And sunke in that dead sea of life
So deep, as he did then death's waters sup;
But that the Corke of Title boy'd him up.

21 *space:* number of years.   **22** *act:* conduct.

23 *Or masked man, if valu'd by his face:* The notion that the face is a mask that hides a man's real personality is not uncommon in Elizabethan and Jacobean literature.

24 *fact:* true nature.

25 *Here's one out-liv'd his Peeres:* Jonson describes a public figure (probably the barrister, Sir Edward Coke) whose life has been long and troublesome, contrasting it with the brief perfection of Morison's.

33 The second turn gives a short biography of the public figure named in the preceding stanza, and shows his progress to corruption.

The Counter-turne

Alas, but Morison fell young:
Hee never fell, thou fall'st, my tongue.
45 Hee stood, a Souldier to the last right end,
A perfect Patriot, and a noble friend,
But most, a vertuous Sonne.
All Offices were done
By him, so ample, full, and round,
50 In weight, in measure, number, sound,
As though his age imperfect might appeare,
His life was of Humanitie the Spheare.

The Stand

Goe now, and tell out dayes summ'd up with feares,
And make them yeares;
55 Produce thy masse of miseries on the Stage,
To swell thine age;
Repeat of things a throng,
To shew thou hast beene long,
Not liv'd; for Life doth her great actions spell,
60 By what was done and wrought
In season, and so brought
To light: her measures are, how well
Each syllab'e answer'd, and was form'd, how faire;
These make the lines of life, and that's her ayre.

The Turne

65 It is not growing like a tree
In bulke, doth make man better bee;

48 *Offices:* duties.

52 *His life was of Humanitie the Spheare:* Jonson returns to the figure of the circle in lines 9 and 10. The sphere is the perfect figure, the paradigm.

59 *spell:* make known.   **63** *syllab'e:* individual action.

64 *ayre:* distinctive quality.

65-74 The third turn, symbolically placed in the centre of the ode, is perhaps the most perfect summing up of Jonson's humanistic philosophy; it is usually printed as a separate lyric. The aphoristic reflections are in the spirit of Horace and Martial.

Or standing long an Oake, three hundred yeare,
To fall a logge at last, dry, bald, and seare:
A Lillie of a Day,
70 Is fairer farre, in May,
Although it fall, and die that night;
It was the Plant, and flowre of light.
In small proportions, we just beautie see:
And in short measures, life may perfect bee.

The Counter-turne

75 Call, noble Lucius, then for Wine,
And let thy lookes with gladnesse shine:
Accept this garland, plant it on thy head,
And thinke, nay know, thy Morison's not dead.
Hee leap'd the present age,
80 Possest with holy rage,
To see that bright eternall Day:
Of which we Priests, and Poets say
Such truths, as we expect for happy men,
And there he lives with memorie; and Ben

The Stand

85 Jonson, who sung this of him, e're he went
Himselfe to rest,
Or taste a part of that full joy he meant
To have exprest,
In this bright Asterisme:
90 Where it were friendships schisme,
(Were not his Lucius long with us to tarry)
To separate these twi-
Lights, the Dioscuri;
And keepe the one halfe from his Harry.

84 In ending the Counter-turn in the middle of a proper name Jonson
is imitating Pindar's run-on lines and stanzas. So also lines 92-3.
89 *Asterisme:* constellation.   **92-3** *twi-Lights:* twin stars.
93 *Dioscuri:* Castor and Pollux, the heavenly twins.

95 But fate doth so alternate the designe,
    Whilst that in heav'n, this light on earth must shine.

The Turne

    And shine as you exalted are;
    Two names of friendship, but one Starre:
    Of hearts the union. And those not by chance
100 Made, or indentur'd, or leas'd out t⟨o⟩ 'advance
    The profits for a time.
    No pleasures vaine did chime,
    Of rimes, or ryots, at your feasts,
    Orgies of drinke, or fain'd protests:
105 But simple love of greatnesse, and of good;
    That knits brave minds, and manners, more then blood.

The Counter-turne

    This made you first to know the Why
    You lik'd, then after, to apply
    That liking; and approach so one the tother,
110 Till either grew a portion of the other:
    Each stiled, by his end,
    The Copie of his friend.
    You liv'd to be the great surnames,
    And titles, by which all made claimes
115 Unto the Vertue. Nothing perfect done,
    But as a CARY, or a MORISON.

The Stand

    And such a force the faire example had,
    As they that saw
    The good, and durst not practise it, were glad
120 That such a Law
    Was left yet to Man-kind;
    Where they might read, and find
    Friendship, in deed, was written, not in words:
    And with the heart, not pen,

125   Of two so early men,
        Whose lines her rowles were, and records.
        Who, e're the first downe bloomed on the chin,
        Had sow'd these fruits, and got the harvest in.

    125 *so early:* such young.   **126** *rowles:* rolls.

Abraham Cowley

THE reputation of Cowley stood higher in his day than at any time since. His influence is now seen principally in his development of the ode as a genus of poetry capable of infinite modification and flexibility. The richness of the ode's variety is realized only in the eighteenth and nineteenth centuries in the hands of transitional and romantic poets, such as Gray, Collins, Wordsworth, Shelley, Keats and Tennyson.

Cowley was born in London, and educated at Westminster School and Trinity College, Cambridge. As a Royalist he became an exile in France during the Commonwealth, and was secretary to Queen Henrietta Maria in Paris. He is buried in Westminster Abbey. His writings in English and Latin were collected posthumously in 1668, by Thomas Sprat, the historian of the Royal Society, and later Dean of Westminster and Bishop of Rochester, who supplied a biography. *The Mistress* had been published in 1647, and there were volumes of verses and translations in 1656 and 1663. That he was widely read is shown by a pirated edition in Dublin called *The Iron Age* in which many spurious poems were fathered upon him. He refers to them in his Preface to *Verses Written on Several Occasions* (1663), and says that he commenced writing at the age of ten. Many of his earlier works were destroyed, including an account of the Civil War.

Cowley described the nature of his Pindaric odes in "The Resurrection", and feared that they might be misunderstood: "The digressions are many, and sudden. . . . The Figures are unusual and bold, even to Temerity. . . . The Numbers are various and irregular, and sometimes (especially some of the long ones) seem harsh and uncouth" (Preface, 1663). He was self-critical, but more learned than naturally gifted. Dr. Johnson, in his *Lives of the Poets*, charges the late metaphysicals with "perverseness of industry", preferring novelty to naturalness and singularity to careful diction. Cowley's excessive analysis, he says, breaks "every image into fragments", dissecting "a sun-beam with a prism"; but he praises Cowley's agility of mind. His merit was "not to shew precisely what Pindar spoke, but his manner of speaking". Johnson does not share Sprat's enthusiasm for Cowley's diction as "chiefly to be preferred for its near affinity to prose".

After the Restoration, Cowley lived modestly in retirement on the Thames, enjoying the literary solitude he once planned to find by emigrating to America. In his desire for peace of mind, as well as his art, he was a disciple of Horace.

THE PRAISE OF PINDAR

COWLEY was not an imitator, but an adapter of Pindar, in what resembles free verse. He invented the irregular English ode (without Pindar's balanced triadic structure); in time this culminated in the odes of Wordsworth on "Intimations of Immortality" and Tennyson on "The Death of the Duke of Wellington". In the hands of minor poets, this difficult form became licentious and artificial; but Dryden, Milton, Gray and Collins all achieved success in it. Cowley wrote fifteen Pindarics, the style of which is rhapsodic, even baroque. Crashaw, with whom he made literary acquaintanceship at Cambridge, may have influenced his style. This ode, published in 1656, is a re-working (not imitation) of Horace's encomium of Pindar's tempestuousness in *Odes* IV. 2, which Cowley unhappily accepted as a just estimate of the Greek poet. His talent did not compass the range of Pindar's imagination; but he supplied the deficiency with fancy, wit, dialectic and classical scholarship, which partly shows in Cowley's conventional choice of epithets. The text of the poem is from A. R. Waller's *Poems* of Abraham Cowley (Cambridge, 1905). The ode is cast in a form that is not Horatian, but conveys the critical ideas of Horace about Pindar. These are actually unsound; Pindar was not like a swollen river that "rages boundless through the plain"; his metrical skill was superbly controlled, expressed in language sublime and metaphorical.

> Pindar is imitable by none;
>   The Phoenix Pindar is a vast Species alone.
> Who e're but Daedalus with waxen wings could fly
> And neither sink too low, nor soar too high?
> 5   What could he who follow'd claim,
> But of vain boldness the unhappy fame.
>   And by his fall a Sea to name?

2 *The Phoenix Pindar:* The reference is to the fabulous Egyptian bird that lived for five centuries and immolated itself on a fire of aromatic wood, from the ashes of which rose its offspring. The image which is Cowley's, not Horace's, implies that Pindar is a rare phenomenon among poets.

3 *Daedalus:* the Athenian sculptor, who lived in Crete to escape the sentence of death for the murder of his nephew. The name means "cunning craftsman". He constructed the labyrinth at Cnossos, and flew with his son over the Aegean sea, using artificial wings attached with wax.

5 *he who follow'd:* Icarus, the son of Daedalus.

7 *And by his fall a Sea to name:* Approaching too near the sun, Icarus lost his wings by the melting of the wax, and was drowned, the sea henceforth being known as Mare Icareum.

Pindars unnavigable Song
Like a swoln Flood from some steep Mountain pours along,
10   The Ocean meets with such a Voice
From his enlarged Mouth, as drowns the Oceans noise.

So Pindar does new Words and Figures roul
Down his impetuous Dithyrambique Tide,
          Which in no Channel deigns t'abide,
15   Which neither Banks nor Dikes controul.
          Whether th' Immortal Gods he sings
          In a no less Immortal strain,
Or the great Acts of God-descended Kings,
Who in his Numbers still survive and Reign.
20   Each rich embroidered Line,
     Which their triumphant Brows around,
          By his sacred Hand is bound,
Does all their starry Diadems outshine.

Whether at Pisa's race he please
25 To carve in polisht Verse the Conque'rors Images,

8 *Pindars unnavigable Song:* Cowley, in his notes, speaks of Pindar's
"Poetical Fury", but adds that Horace elsewhere calls him a "Fountain" of
invention.

13 *Dithyrambique Tide:* The Dithyramb was a flute-accompanied hymn
dance in honour of Dionysus (Bacchus). It was perfected at Corinth by
Arion, who divided the hymn into strophe and antistrophe (later abolished
by Lasos). It was characterized by bold, inspired language and frequent
changes of rhythm. One of the prizes awarded to the poet was an ox.

15 *Banks nor Dikes:* Cowley's note adds that banks are natural, dikes
artificial; meaning that neither Nature nor Art could control Pindar's
"half-mad" enthusiasm.

21-3 Cowley refers to the use by ancient kings of "diadems", instead of
crowns. The word comes from Greek διαδεῖν (to bind about), because a
white ribbon, studded with gems, was worn about the head of the monarch.

24 *Pisa:* chief town in the centre of Elis, a province of the Peloponnese,
and not far from Olympia and the river Alphaeus. There was great rivalry
in this part of the world for the presidency of the Olympian games.

25 *the Conque'rors Images:* Victors at the Games were not only crowned
with garlands of wild olive, but had statues erected to them.

Whether the Swift, the Skilful, or the Strong,
Be crowned in his Nimble, Artful, Vigorous Song:
Whether some brave young man's untimely fate
In words worth Dying for he celebrate,
30   Such mournful, and such pleasing words,
As joy to' his Mothers and his Mistress grief affords:
              He bids him Live and Grow in fame,
              Among the Stars he sticks his Name:
The Grave can but the Dross of him devour,
35   So small is Deaths, so great the Poets power.

Lo, how th'obsequious Wind, and swelling Ayr
              The Theban Swan does upwards bear
Into the walks of Clouds, where he does play,
And with the extended Wings opens his liquid way.
40   Whilst, alas, my tim'erous Muse
              Unambitious tracks pursues;
              Does with weak unballast wings,
              About the mossy Brooks and Springs;
              About the Trees new-blossom'ed Heads,
45   About the Gardens painted Beds,

28-33 Cowley refers to the threnodies or funeral elegies of Pindar, which are lost.

37 *The Theban Swan:* Pindar. Horace has *Dircaean* Swan. Swans were supposed to sing most beautifully before they died (hence swan-song). In the *Greek Anthology* there is a reference to "Sweet-tongued Pindar, the Heliconian Swan of Thebes". Poets called themselves the Swans of the Muses and Apollo.

39 *liquid way:* a metaphysical image of a wheeling bird soaring effortlessly above the clouds.

40-1 *my tim'erous Muse/Unambitious tracks pursues:* Horace modestly compared himself to a honey-bee, rather than a soaring swan, futilely trying to imitate Pindar. Cowley greatly extends the comparison, and omits the last seven stanzas of Horace's ode, in which the poet commemorates the victory of Augustus over the Sygambri in Germany, and pays a compliment to Julius Antonius, who introduced him to the Emperor.

42 *unballast:* unsteady.

About the Fields and flowry Meads,
And all inferior beauteous things
Like the laborious Bee,
For little drops of Honey flee,
50 And there with Humble Sweets contents her Industrie.

TO MR. HOBS

THOMAS HOBBES (1588-1679), son of a poor country parson, was edu-
cated at Magdalen College, Oxford, and disapproved of his university
training, despite ambitions to be a classical scholar. His life-long association
with the influential Lord Cavendish brought him into contact with the
leading intellectuals of his age, both in England and France. He became a
philosopher in middle age after studying mathematics and science, and
visiting Galileo in Italy. While exiled in France, he became the tutor of
the future Charles II, and wrote his principal work *Leviathan*. He was a
great controversialist, especially after the Restoration; hence the reference
to the shield of his Reason in line 70. Cowley knew him intimately and
admired his intellectual scope; the tribute to Hobbes is one of his best odes.

Vast Bodies of Philosophie
I oft have seen, and read,
But all are Bodies Dead,
Or Bodies by Art fashioned;
5   I never yet the Living Soul could see,
But in thy Books and Thee.
'Tis onely God can know
Whether the fair Idea thou dost show
Agree intirely with his own or no.
10   This I dare boldly tell,
'Tis so like Truth 'twill serve our turn as well.
Just, as in Nature thy Proportions be,
As full of Concord their Varietie,
As firm the parts upon their Center rest,

8 *the fair Idea:* the eternal principle, using the word *idea* in the Platonic
sense.

11 *'Tis so like Truth 'twill serve our turn as well:* i.e. The principles en-
unciated by Hobbes are as near to God's concept of objective truth as it is
possible for humans to come.

15 And all so Solid are that they at least
    As much as Nature, Emptiness detest.

    Long did the mighty Stagirite retain
    The universal Intellectual reign,
    Saw his own Countreys short-lived Leopard slain;
20 The stronger Roman-Eagle did out-fly,
    Oftner renewed his Age, and saw that Dy.
    Mecha it self, in spite of Mahumet possest,
    And chas'ed by a wild Deluge from the East,
    His Monarchy new planted in the West.
25 But as in time each great imperial race
    Degenerates, and gives some new one place:
            So did this noble Empire wast,
            Sunk by degrees from glories past,
    And in the School-mens hands it perisht quite at last.
30   Then nought but Words it grew,
            And those all Barb'arous too.
        It perisht, and it vanisht there,
    The Life and Soul breath'd out, became but empty Air.

12-16 A reference to Hobbes's deterministic universe and mechanistic
psychology. He was not a good metaphysician. T. S. Eliot calls *Leviathian*
"an adumbration of the universe of material atoms regulated by laws of
motion which formed the scientific view of the world from Newton to
Einstein".

16 Cf. "Nature abhors a vacuum."

17 *the mighty Stagirite:* Aristotle, who was born at Stagira in Macedonia.

19 *Saw his own Countreys short-lived Leopard slain:* a reference to the short
life of Alexander's Grecian Empire, which was depicted as a Leopard in the
vision of *Daniel,* vii, 6.

20 *The stronger Roman-Eagle did out-fly:* Cowley is describing the longe-
vity of Aristotle's philosophy, which outlived the Roman Empire, as well
as the Greek.

22-4 *Mecha it self:* Mecca was the birthplace of Mahomet. Aristotle's
works were preserved by the Arabs, and influenced their thinking, even
after they were overrun by the Turks and transferred their power to the
West.

29 *the School-mens hands:* the scholastic philosophers, disciples of Thomas
Aquinas, who founded the University of Paris, which was dedicated to the
preservation of Aristotle's philosophy, especially his principles of logic.

The Fields which answer'd well the Ancients Plow,
35 Spent and out-worn return no Harvest now,
In barren Age wild and unglorious lie,
        And boast of past Fertilitie,
The poor relief of Present Povertie.
        Food and Fruit we now must want
40   Unless new Lands we plant.
We break up Tombs with Sacrilegious hands;
        Old Rubbish we remove;
To walk in Ruines, like vain Ghosts, we love,
        And with fond Divining Wands
45   We search among the Dead
        For Treasures Buried,
Whilst still the Liberal Earth does hold
So many Virgin Mines of undiscover'ed Gold.

The Baltique, Euxin, and the Caspian,
50 And slender-limb'ed Mediterrrean,
Seem narrow Creeks to Thee, and only fit
For the poor wretched Fisher-boats of Wit
Thy nobler Vessel the vast Ocean tries,
        And nothing sees but Seas and Skies,
55   Till unknown Regions it descries,
Thou great Columbus of the Golden Lands of new Philo-
        sophies.
        Thy task was harder much then his,
        For thy learn'd America is

34-48 This stanza is a view of the state of learning in the Renaissanc e with its dependence on the knowledge of the past. Cowley regards philosophy as exhausted until the advent of seventeenth-century scientific thinkers.

44 *Divining Wands:* The *virgula divina* or divining two-forked rod of ancient times was used for detecting underground water, ores or treasure.

49 *Euxin:* The Black Sea.

49-52 The four seas mentioned were those principally navigated in ancient times. The Atlantic was seldom visited, except along the European or African coast.

53-6 Hobbes is seen as an intellectual pioneer, with vast horizons, like Columbus in another sphere.

     Not onely found out first by Thee,
60 And rudely left to Future Industrie,
     But thy Eloquence and thy Wit,
Has planted, peopled, built, and civiliz'd it.

     I little thought before,
    (Nor being my own self so poor
65   Could comprehend so vast a store)
    That all the Wardrobe of rich Eloquence,
     Could have afforded half enuff,
     Of bright, of new, and lasting stuff,
To cloath the mighty Limbs of thy Gigantique Sence.
70 Thy solid Reason like the shield from heaven
       To the Trojan Heroe given,
Too strong to take a mark from any mortal dart,
Yet shines, with Gold and Gems in every part,
And Wonders on it grave'd by the learn'd hand of Art,
75   A shield that gives delight
     Even to the enemies sight,
Then when they're sure to lose the Combat by't.

    Nor can the Snow which now cold Age does shed
     Upon thy reverend Head,
80 Quench or allay the noble Fires within,
     But all which thou hast bin,
     And all that Youth can be thou'rt yet,
     So fully still dost Thou

61-2 Hobbes not only opened a new world, but civilized it by his genius as a writer.

63-9 Cowley wonders at the unbelievable resources of language to express the new philosophical ideas.

69 *The mighty Limbs of thy Gigantique Sence:* a physical image of the intellect as Leviathan, the sea monster, mentioned in the Old Testament. It was overcome by Baal in the Ugarit or Phoenician creation legends.

70-7 *the shield from heaven/To the Trojan Heroe given:* the huge impenetrable shield of Æneas, which his mother Venus obtained from Vulcan. The sword of Turnus broke like ice upon it (*Æneid,* Books VIII and XII). On the shield was engraved the history of the Romans. Cowley compares the power of Reason to it.

Enjoy the Manhood, and the Bloom of Wit,
85   And all the Natural Heat, but not the Feaver too.
So Contraries on Ætna's top conspire,
Here Hoary Frosts, and by them breaks out Fire.
A secure peace the faithful Neighbors keep,
Th' emboldned Snow next to the Flame does sleep,
90   And if we weigh, like Thee,
          Nature, and Causes, we shall see
          That thus it needs must be,
To things Immortal Time can do no wrong,
And that which never is to Dye, for ever must be Young.

85 *The Feaver:* unreasonable enthusiasm.

86 *So Contraries on Ætna's top conspire:* the flames of eruption surrounded by the snowy summit. The image occurs in Tacitus's description of Mount Libanus in his *Annals*.

91 *Nature, and Causes:* natural cause and effect, which Hobbes said survive time, because matter is indestructible.

Ben Jonson

TO HEAVEN

IMAGERY is not, with classical poets, the indispensable means of conveying ideas. They rely more on balance, contrast, proportion; organized control of language and dexterity in the handling of metrical effects. In this ode we glimpse the devout Jonson, whose language has a biblical simplicity.

Good, and great God, can I not thinke of thee,
    But it must, straight, my melancholy bee?
Is it interpreted in me disease,
    That, laden with my sinnes, I seeke for ease?
5   O, be thou witnesse, that the reynes dost know,
    And hearts of all, if I be sad for show,
And judge me after: if I dare pretend
    To ought but grace, or ayme at other end.

5 *reynes:* reins or kidneys, thought in the Middle Ages and later to be the source of the feelings.

As thou art all, so be thou all to mee,
10   First, midst, and last, converted one, and three;
My faith, my hope, my love: and in this state,
        My judge, my witnesse, and my advocate.
Where have I beene this while exil'd from thee?
        And whither rap'd, now thou but stoup'st to mee?
15   Dwell, dwell here still: O, being every-where,
        How can I doubt to finde thee ever, here?
I know my state, both full of shame, and scorne,
        Conceiv'd in sinne, and unto labour borne,
Standing with feare, and must with horror fall,
20   And destin'd unto judgement, after all.
I feele my griefes too, and there scarce is ground,
        Upon my flesh t⟨o⟩' inflict another wound.
Yet dare I not complaine, or wish for death
        With holy Paul, lest it be thought the breath
25   Of discontent; or that these prayers bee
        For werinesse of life, not love of thee.

10 *converted:* made.   **14** *rap'd:* carried off.
24 *With holy Paul:* See *Romans* vii, 24; this chapter may have suggested
the poem to Jonson; but Paul is not, at the end, wishing for physical death.
25 *prayers:* The word is here disyllabic.

TO HIMSELF

IN this experiment, Jonson skilfully modulates iambic trimeters with initial
trochees, and ends his regular stanzas with hexameters. This gives the ode
the appearance of Pindaric impetuosity, but underneath there is the moral
fervour and epigrammatic ease of Horace. Jonson favoured the Horatian
ode, because he liked its level flight and sober grace of movement. Here he
cultivates Horace's economy of phrase, mythological allusions and personal
touches. The vividness and self-exhortation are Jonson's own.

Where do'st thou carelesse lie,
        Buried in ease and sloth?
Knowledge, that sleepes, doth die;
And this Securitie,
5   It is the common Moath,
That eats on wits, and Arts, and ⟨oft⟩ destroyes them both.

Are all the' Aonian springs
  Dri'd up? lyes Thespia wast?
Doth Clarius Harp want strings,
10 That not a Nymph now sings?
  Or droop they as disgrac't,
To see their Seats and Bowers by chattring Pies defac't?

If hence thy silence be,
  As 'tis too just a cause;
15 Let this thought quicken thee,
  Minds that are great and free,
  Should not on fortune pause,
'Tis crowne enough to vertue still, her owne applause.

What though the greedie Frie
20 Be taken with false Baytes
Of worded Balladrie,
And thinke it Poesie?
  They die with their conceits,
And only pitious scorne, upon their folly waites.

25 Then take in hand thy Lyre,
  Strike in thy proper straine,
With Japhets lyne, aspire
Sols Chariot for new fire,

7 *Aonian springs:* haunt of the Muses. Aonia was the earlier name of Boeotia, named after Aon, son of Neptune, who came to the region from Apulia in the age of Cadmus.

8 *Thespia:* a town at the foot of Mount Helicon, named after Thespia, daughter of Asopus.

9 *Clarius:* the surname of Apollo, who had an oracle at Claros, a town of Iona, founded by the weeping Manto, daughter of Tiresias, when a fugitive from Thebes.

12 *chattring Pies:* i.e. magpies, the poetic rivals of Jonson. The reference is from Pindar's Olympian Ode II, strophe 5.

19 *Frie:* immature fish.

21 *worded:* verbose.

27 *Japhet:* Japetus, called by the Greeks "the father of all mankind". He married Asia, and was the father of Atlas and Prometheus.

To give the world againe:
30 Who aided him, will thee, the issue of Joves braine.

And since our Daintie age,
Cannot indure reproofe,
Make not thy selfe a Page,
To that strumpet the Stage,
35   But sing high and aloofe,
Safe from the wolves black jaw, and the dull Asses hoofe.

30 *the issue of Joves braine:* Minerva, goddess of wisdom, war and liberal arts.
36 A reference to merciless and stupid critics.

TO HIMSELF, PROVOKED BY THE POOR RECEPTION OF *THE NEW INN*

IN 1629, on the title-page of his comedy, *The New Inn,* Jonson blamed the King's Players for the neglience of their performance and the consequent censure of the public. Most of his later plays were literary dotages, and failures in the theatre. He reacted strongly to public opinion. As a man, he was not without asperity and grossness; but he had many of Horace's qualities as a writer. Pugnacious satire was not, however, in Horace's vein, but Martial's. This satirical ode, in ten-lined stanzas comprising trimeters and pentameters, occasioned many rejoinders, especially from poets who took offence at Jonson's reference to Richard Brome's *The Love-sick Maid,* a play no longer extant, but licensed for performance on February 9, 1629. R. L. Stevenson, in a letter to Sir Edmund Gosse, thought stanzas 2 to 4 unworthy of the rest of this ode.

Come leave the loathed Stage,
And the more loathsome Age,
Where pride and impudence in faction knit,
Usurpe the Chaire of wit:
5 Inditing and arraigning every day,
Something they call a Play.
Let their fastidious vaine
Commission of the braine,
Runne on, and rage, sweat, censure, and condemn:
10 They were not made for thee, lesse thou for them.

8 *Commission:* probably a reference to the Ecclesiastical Court of High Commission, founded by Queen Elizabeth and abolished in 1641.

Say that thou pour'st 'hem wheat,
     And they would Akornes eat:
'Twere simple fury, still thy selfe to wast
     On such as have no taste:
15   To offer them a surfeit of pure bread,
          Whose appetites are dead:
     No, give them Graines their fill,
     Huskes, Draffe to drinke, and swill:
If they love Lees, and leave the lusty Wine,
20   Envy them not, their pallat's with the Swine

     No doubt a mouldy Tale,
          Like Pericles, and stale
As the Shrives crusts, and nasty as his Fish,
     Scraps out of every Dish,
25   Throwne forth and rak'd into the common Tub,
          May keep up the Play Club.
     Broomes sweepings doe as well
     There, as his Masters meale:
For who the relish of these guests will fit,
30   Needs set them but the Almes-basket of wit.

     And much good do't yee then,
          Brave Plush and Velvet men

13 *simple:* mere.

17 *Graines:* the residue of the malt after brewing.

18 *Draffe:* dregs.

21-2 *a mouldy tale,/Like Pericles:* the play, partly by Shakespeare, published in quarto in 1609, but not in the First Folio of 1623.

23 *the Shrives crusts:* the Sheriff's food supplied in prisons.

25 *the common Tub:* refuse basket for leavings after civic feasts, which were given to the poor. Cf. Shakespeare, *Love's Labour's Lost*, V. 1. 33-6.

26 *Play Club:* gambling club.

27 *Broomes sweepings:* The pun is on the name of the playwright Richard Brome, formerly Jonson's servant. Brome's play, *The Love-sick Maid*, also performed by the King's Players, was so successful that a special gift of £2 was sent to the Master of the Revels. Jonson afterwards suppressed this jealous reference to Brome and wrote gratulatory verses to his next play.

Can feed on Orts; and safe in your scoene cloaths,
    Dare quit upon your Oathes
35 The Stagers, and the stage-writes too; your Peers,
    Of stuffing your large eares
    With rage of Commicke socks,
    Wrought upon twenty Blocks;
Which, if they're torne, and foule, and patch'd enough,
40 The Gamesters share your gilt, and you their stuffe.

    Leave things so prostitute,
    And take th'Alcaike Lute;
Or thine owne Horace, or Anacreons Lyre;
    Warme thee by Pindars fire:
45 And though thy Nerves be shrunke, and blood be cold,
    Ere years have made thee old,
    Strike that disdainfull heat
    Throughout, to their defeat:
As curious fooles, and envious of thy straine,
50 May blushing sweare, no Palsi's in thy braine.

33 *Orts:* scraps.   **35** *Stagers:* actors.

37 *Commicke socks: Socci* or footwear of the Greek and Roman actors in comedy.

38 *Blocks:* The wooden moulds on which *socci* were made; also a pun on "blockheads".

40 *Gamesters:* gamblers.   *gilt:* gold paint of the *socci*; also a pun on "guilt".

42 *Alcaike Lute:* the legendary instrument of Alcaeus, the Greek lyric poet of Lesbos, whose metrical mantle descended upon Horace, referred to as the patron of Jonson in the next line. See also *Poetaster* in which Jonson represents himself as Horace.

43 *Anacreons Lyre:* the instrument of Anacreon of Teos (born, middle of sixth century B.C.), a love-poet of *The Greek Anthology.*

44 *Pindars fire:* a reference to the Greek lyrist's "enthusiasm" or warmth of inspiration.

45 *Nerves:* Latin *nervi* meant "sinews"; hence *shrunk* in this context. The meaning is retained in the idiomatic expression "to strain every nerve". In the seventeenth century the word acquired its present medical significance.

49 *curious:* fastidious, difficult to satisfy.

50 *Palsi:* a corruption of *paralysie*, a disease of the nervous system. Only the previous year Jonson had been stricken with paralysis.

But when they heare thee sing
The glories of thy King;
His zeale to God, and his just awe of men,
They may be blood-shaken, then
55 Feele such a flesh-quake to possesse their powers,
That no tun'd Harpe like ours,
In sound of Peace or Warres,
Shall truely hit the Starres
When they shall read the Acts of Charles his Reigne,
60 And see his Chariot triumph 'bove his Waine.

58 *hit the Starres:* an echo of Horace, *Odes* I. 1. 35-6.

59 *Charles his Reigne:* a reference to the new King, Charles I.

60 *Waine:* waggon; also a pun on "wane". The reference is both to the vehicle of Charlemagne, and to the wain of Arcturus, seven stars in the northern constellation Ursa Major.

John Milton

AT A SOLEMN MUSICK

MILTON was a lover of the organ, especially when accompanied by the singing of large choirs. This ode, in alternate-rhyming pentameters, has initial trochees to announce the invocations of the first two lines. The ode speaks of the happy union of music and verse; in juncture they extend the power of the imagination. It is through the marriage of reason and sensibility that the "prophetic strain" is born, and we are returned to the Golden Age celebrated in early Greek poetry. Milton suggests that music originated in Heaven around the throne of God, and brought harmony on earth before the Fall. He hopes that human beings will once more "consent" by their obedience to this eternal concord, and be reunited in the peace of God. The ode has the Pindaric fervour of inspiration, but is cast in Horatian mould.

Blest pair of Sirens, pledges of Heav'ns joy,
Sphear-born harmonious Sisters, Voice, and Vers,
Wed your divine sounds, and mixt power employ
Dead things with inbreath'd sense able to pierce,
5 And to our high-rais'd phantasie present,
That undisturbed Song of pure concent,

5 *phantasie:* imagination.

Ay sung before the saphire-colour'd throne
To him that sits thereon
With Saintly shout, and solemn Jubily,
10 Where the bright Seraphim in burning row
Their loud up-lifted Angel trumpets blow,
And the Cherubick host in thousand quires
Touch their immortal Harps of golden wires,
With those just Spirits that wear victorious Palms,
15 Hymns devout and holy Psalms
Singing everlastingly;
That we on Earth with undiscording voice
May rightly answer that melodious noise;
As once we did, till disproportion'd sin
20 Jarr'd against natures chime, and with harsh din
Broke the fair musick that all creatures made
To their great Lord, whose love their motion sway'd
In perfet Diapason, whilst they stood
In first obedience, and their state of good.
25 O may we soon again renew that Song,
And keep in tune with Heav'n, till God ere long
To his celestial consort us unite,
To live with him, and sing in endles morn of light.

19 *disproportion'd:* ugly, unseemly.

20 *Jarr'd against natures chime:* struck a discordant note.

23 *Diapason:* grand burst of harmony; originally the notes and intervals in the diatonic scale.

27 *consort:* company of musicians.

Robert Herrick

AN ODE TO SIR CLIPSEBIE CREW

THIS poem invites a friend to dinner, with the ease and charm of Horace. Herrick has in mind a similar invitation of Ben Jonson (No. CI of the *Epigrams*). But the touch of Herrick is lighter than Jonson's and his rural conviviality is in the spirit of Michael Drayton's "Merrie England". He is a master of the short line and the neatly-turned stanza, which give to his odes a freshness and delicacy unequalled in English verse. His spontaneity is deceptive; it is the result of skilful pruning and emulation of Horace.

Self-criticism and faultless selection became the watchword, not only of
Herrick, but of most of the classical followers of Jonson. Sir Clipsebie Crew
(1599-1648), a man of taste and friend of John Evelyn, was educated at St.
John's College, Cambridge, and Lincoln's Inn; he became a Member of
Parliament.

> Here we securely live, and eate
>   The Creame of meat;
> And keep eternal fires,
> By which we sit, and doe Divine
> 5   As Wine
>   And Rage inspires.
>
> If full we charme; then call upon
>   Anacreon
> To grace the frantick Thyrse:
> 10 And having drunk, we raise a shout
>   Throughout
>   To praise his Verse.
>
> Then cause we Horace to be read,
>   Which sung, or seyd,
> 15 A Goblet, to the brim,
> Of Lyrick Wine, both swell'd and crown'd,
>   A Round
>   We quaffe to him.
>
> Thus, thus, we live, and spend the houres
> 20   In Wine and Flowers:
> And make the frollick yeere,
> The Month, the Week, the instant Day
>   To stay
>   The longer here.

1 *securely:* free from care.

3 *eternal fires:* A recollection of Martial, X. 47. 4.

4 *Divine:* think, day-dream.   6 *Rage:* mood, sudden feeling.

7 *charme:* Sing or play on a musical instrument.

8 *Anacreon:* Greek poet of love and wine.

9 *the frantick Thyrse:* The Thyrsus was the staff of Dionysus (Bacchus)
tipped with a fir-cone, and wreathed with ivy and vine-leaves. *Frantick*
is a transferred epithet, meaning "wild" or "frenzied".

22 *instant:* immediate, present.

25 Come then, brave Knight, and see the Cell
        Wherein I dwell;
    And my Enchantments too;
    Which Love and noble freedome is;
            And this
30   Shall fetter you.

    Take Horse, and come; or be so kind,
        To send your mind
    (Though but in Numbers few)
    And I shall think I have the heart,
35   Or part
        Of Clipseby Crew.

30 *fetter:* "bind fast", looking back to the word *Enchantments.*
33 *Numbers:* verses.

THE COUNTRY LIFE, TO THE HONOURED MR. ENDIMION PORTER, GROOME OF THE BED-CHAMBER TO HIS MAJESTY

ENDYMION PORTER (1587-1649), a Gloucestershire Royalist, was brought up in Spain, and through the Duke of Buckingham entered the service of Charles I, with a pension of £500 a year. He lost his property during the Civil War and died in poverty in the same year as his monarch. He was a minor poet and patron of the arts, and his friendship with Rubens and Van Dyck enabled him to build up the King's collection of pictures. He also secured the Arundel collection of paintings from Spain. In "The Country Life" the moral values are inspired by Horace, *Odes* I. 1.; but there are suggestions of pictorial idealization in the manner of Vergil's *Eclogues* and *Georgics.* This is an example of the didactic ode of fruitful leisure. Endymion Porter seemed to Herrick a man, like Horace, not only of eclectic taste but of rich personality, country-loving, kindly and tolerant.

    Sweet Country life, to such unknown,
    Whose lives are others, not their own!
    But serving Courts, and Cities, be
    Less happy, less enjoying thee.
5   Thou never Plow'st the Oceans foame
    To seek, and bring rough Pepper home:

6 *rough Pepper:* The epithet probably refers to the biting, pungent property of the condiment, not to a brand.

Nor to the Eastern Ind dost rove
To bring from thence the scorched Clove.
Nor, with the losse of thy lov'd rest,
10 Bring'st home the Ingot from the West.
No, thy Ambition's Master-piece
Flies no thought higher then a fleece:
Or how to pay thy Hinds, and cleere
All scores; and so to end the yeere:
15 But walk'st about thine own dear bounds,
Not envying others larger grounds:
For well thou know'st, 'tis not th'extent
Of Land makes life, but sweet content.
When now the Cock (the Plow-mans Horne)
20 Calls forth the lilly-wristed Morne;
Then to thy corn-fields thou dost goe,
Which though well soyl'd, yet thou dost know,
That the best compost for the Lands
Is the wise Masters Feet, and Hands.
25 There at the Plough thou find'st thy Teame,
With a Hind whistling there to them:
And cheer'st them up, by singing how
The Kingdoms portion is the Plow.
This done, then to th'enameld Meads
30 Thou go'st; and as thy foot there treads,
Thou seest a present God-like Power
Imprinted in each Herbe and Flower:
And smell'st the breath of great-ey'd Kine,
Sweet as the blossomes of the Vine.
35 Here thou behold'st thy large sleek Neat
Unto the Dew-laps up in meat:

13 *Hinds:* servants.

20 *lilly-wristed:* an image emphasizing the whiteness of morning frost.

23-4 Probably a reference to the proverb "Master's footsteps fatten the soil" (L. C. Martin).

28 *The Kingdoms portion is the Plow:* In 1601 Lord Cecil said: "whosoever doth not maintain the Plough destroys the Kingdom" (*Journal of House of Lords and Commons,* 1693).

35 *Neat:* cattle.

And, as thou look'st, the wanton Steere,
The Heifer, Cow, and Oxe draw neere
To make a pleasing pastime there.
40   These seen, thou go'st to view thy flocks
Of sheep, (safe from the Wolfe and Fox)
And find'st their bellies there as full
Of short sweet grasse, as backs with wool.
And leav'st them (as they feed and fill)
45   A Shepherd piping on a hill.
For Sports, for Pagentrie, and Playes,
Thou hast thy Eves, and Holydayes:
On which the young men and maids meet,
To exercise their dancing feet:
50   Tripping the comely country round,
With Daffadils and Daisies crown'd.
Thy Wakes, thy Quintels, here thou hast,
Thy May-poles too with Garlands grac't:
Thy Morris-dance; thy Whitsun-ale;
55   Thy Sheering-feast, which never faile.
Thy Harvest home; thy Wassaile bowle,
That's tost up after Fox i'th'Hole.
Thy Mummeries; thy Twelfe-tide Kings
And Queenes; thy Christmas revellings:
60   Thy Nut-browne mirth; thy Russet wit;
And no man payes too deare for it.

52 *Wakes:* village sports, dancing, etc., held at an annual festival of the parish, usually to commemorate the patron saint of the local church. *Quintels:* variant of *quintain.* This was a fixed or movable target of some sort to tilt at; a favourite sport at weddings.

54 *Whitsun-ale:* festival at Whitsuntide.

56 *Harvest home:* merry-making to celebrate the homing of the corn. *Wassaile bowle:* loving-cup from which healths are drunk.

57 *Fox i'th'Hole:* a children's game involving hopping on one leg.

58 *Mummeries:* dumb-shows, a popular form of folk acting.　　*Twelfe-tide Kings/And Queenes:* At the season of Epiphany, January 6, when the Christmas festivities ended, Kings and Queens were chosen for the celebration.

60 *Nut-browne mirth:* country amusement.　　*Russet wit:* folk pleasantry. Russet was a homespun woollen cloth used for peasant clothes.

> To these, thou hast thy times to goe
> And trace the Hare i'th'trecherous Snow:
> Thy witty wiles to draw, and get
> 65   The Larke into the Trammell net:
> Thou hast thy Cockrood, and thy Glade
> To take the precious Phesant made:
> Thy Lime-twigs, Snares, and Pit-falls then
> To catch the pilfring Birds, not Men.
> 70   O happy life! if that their good
> The Husbandmen but understood!
> Who all the day themselves doe please,
> And Younglings, with such sports as these.
> And lying down, have nought t'affright
> 75   Sweet sleep, that makes more short the night.
> *Caetera desunt—*

64 *witty wiles:* clever tricks.

65 *Trammell net:* Originally, a fishing net; later, one used for fowling.

66 *Cockrood:* Usually *cockroad* or *cockshoot*. This was a broad way in a glade of trees into which a pheasant might dart, a net being placed for snaring across the opening.

68 *Pit-falls:* traps for birds, consisting of a trapdoor over a cavity or hollow in the ground.

70-1 From Vergil's *Georgics*, II. 458.

75 Suggested by Martial, X. 47. 11.

AN ODE FOR BEN JONSON

OF the three poems on Jonson, this is the best known and most shapely. Jonson is here honoured as a "wit", which probably means for his "acuteness of judgment" and "readiness in response". In poetry the word meant "invention". Lines 15-20 extol the master's self-restraint and economy of phrase, of which this slight ode is an admirable example.

> Ah Ben!
> Say how, or when
> Shall we thy Guests
> Meet at those Lyrick Feasts,

5   Made at the Sun,
  The Dog, the triple Tunne?
 Where we such clusters had,
As made us nobly wild, not mad;
 And yet each Verse of thine
10 Out-did the meate, out-did the frolick wine.

   My Ben
  Or come agen:
  Or send to us
 Thy wits great over-plus;
15 But teach us yet
 Wisely to husband it;
 Lest we that Tallent spend:
And having once brought to an end
 That precious stock; the store
20 Of such a wit the world sho'd have no more.

5-6 *the Sun,/The Dog, the triple Tunne:* names of three London inns where Jonson held his poetry evenings, and presided as a kind of literary dictator. From their acceptance at these meetings, his admirers came to be known as the "Sons of Ben".

7 *clusters:* gatherings.

Andrew Marvell

THIS reserved and, in his own day, little-known poet was born in Yorkshire, fourth child of the Anglican Rector of Holderness, who in 1624 became Headmaster of the Grammar School at Hull. Marvell was educated at Trinity College, Cambridge, where he registered at the age of twelve, and graduated six years later, after contributing with Cowley and Crashaw to *Musa Cantabrigiensis.* His father was drowned in the Humber in 1640; from 1642 to 1646 Marvell travelled in Holland, France, Switzerland, Italy and Spain acquiring four languages. Marvell's culture is European, in the wide sense, not Puritan or insular. Most of his verse, which he made no attempt to publish, was written before 1650, when he joined the Civil War commander, Lord Fairfax, at Appleton House in Yorkshire, as tutor to his daughter. The two years spent in these country surroundings were fruitful of some of his best poetry; they were followed by a period at Eton as tutor to a ward of Oliver Cromwell, until in 1657 he joined Milton in the Latin secretaryship of the Commonwealth.

The rest of Marvell's life was spent in public office, and as Member of Parliament for Hull, his only literary work at this time being the satires and political controversies. One of the wisest things he said was about reformers: "Men may spare their pains where Nature is at work, and the world will not go faster for our driving . . . all things happen in their best and proper time, without any need of officiousness." In his cottage at Highgate he greatly enjoyed solitude and privacy. His poems were posthumously published in 1681, but his reputation was unsung until the end of the eighteenth century. Not only were Marvell's Latin poems the greatest of the time, but his knowledge and use of the Bible was scarcely less than Milton's.

Thomas Cooke's edition of Marvell (1726) contains the earliest biography. Marvell's two parts of *The Rehearsal Transprosed* (1672-3), prose works on religious toleration, much influenced Swift's *Tale of a Tub*. The texts of the poems are from Hugh Macdonald's edition of 1952 (a reprint of the 1681 collection) for the "Muses Library".

AN HORATIAN ODE UPON CROMWEL'S RETURN FROM IRELAND

DR. JOHNSON, to whom Marvell was practically unknown as a poet, said of the regular ode: "The great pleasure of verse arises from the known measure of the lines, and uniform structure of the stanzas, by which the voice is regulated, and the memory relieved" (Life of Cowley). This plea for Horatian regularity of structure would have appealed to Marvell, whose ode upon Cromwell in four-lined iambic stanzas (two tetrameters followed by two trimeters) is a clean dry-point portrait, one of the most polished in the language. Though the poem has many conceits, its conception of the Protector as a national, even divine, mediator, is dignified. Cromwell returned from Ireland late in May 1650, to begin his Scottish campaign in July of the same year. The ode seems, therefore, to have been written in June 1650, just before Marvell's sojourn with Lord Fairfax; but it was not printed until 1776. There are several recollections from Lucan's *Pharsalia*, as translated by Thomas May.

> The forward Youth that would appear
> Must now forsake his Muses dear,
>   Nor in the Shadows sing
>   His Numbers languishing.
> 5 'Tis time to leave the Books in dust,
>   And oyl th' unused Armours rust,

Removing from the Wall
The Corslet of the Hall.
So restless Cromwel could not cease
10   In the inglorious Arts of Peace,
But through adventrous War
Urged his active Star.
And, like the three fork'd Lightning, first
Breaking the Clouds where it was nurst,
15   Did thorough his own Side
His fiery way divide.
For 'tis all one to Courage high
The Emulous or Enemy;
And with such to inclose
20   Is more than to oppose.
Then burning through the Air he went,
And Pallaces and Temples rent:
And Caesars head at last
Did through his Laurels blast.
25   'Tis Madness to resist or blame
The force of angry Heavens flame:
And, if we would speak true,
Much to the Man is due.
Who, from his private Gardens, where
30   He liv'd reserved and austere,
As if his highest plot
To plant the Bergamot,
Could by industrious Valour climbe
To ruine the great Work of Time,
35   And cast the Kingdome old
Into another Mold.

13-20 This passage seems to refer to Cromwell's initial struggle within
his own party (cf. line 15, *his own side*). *Emulous* (line 18) may mean "rivals
for power"; and *to inclose* "to restrain".

24 *Did through his Laurels blast:* an echo of "lightning blasteth not the
Laurell tree" (Philemon Holland, *Pliny* 1601).

32 *Bergamot:* a well-known variety of pear, probably from northern
Italy.

Though Justice against Fate complain,
And plead the antient Rights in vain:
   But those do hold or break
40   As Men are strong or weak.
Nature that hateth emptiness,
Allows of penetration less:
   And therefore must make room
   Where greater Spirits come.
45   What Field of all the Civil Wars,
Where his were not the deepest Scars?
   And Hampton shows what part
   He had of wiser Art.
Where, twining subtile fears with hope,
50   He wove a Net of such a scope,
   That Charles himself might chase
   To Caresbrooks narrow case.
That thence the Royal Actor born
The Tragick Scaffold might adorn:
55   While round the armed Bands
   Did clap their bloody hands.
He nothing common did or mean
Upon that memorable Scene:
   But with his keener Eye
60   The Axes edge did try:
Nor call'd the Gods with vulgar spight
To vindicate his helpless Right,
   But bow'd his comely Head,
   Down as upon a Bed.

42 *penetration:* the attempted occupation of space by two bodies. Research on the properties of a vacuum had recently been conducted by Pascal.

47-52 On November 11, 1647, Charles I fled from Hampton Court to Carisbrooke. Marvell holds the disputed theory that Cromwell thought it wise to let him do so; hence the phrase "wiser Art" (line 48).

52 *case:* "cage" has been suggested; but the meaning is "plight".

57 *He:* i.e. Charles I (the "Royal Actor"), whose conduct is now considered.

59 *keener Eye:* Note the play on "keener" with reference to the "Axes edge". Charles was executed on January 30, 1649.

65 This was that memorable Hour
Which first assur'd the forced Pow'r.
So when they did design
The Capitols first Line,
A bleeding Head where they begun,
70 Did fright the Architects to run;
And yet in that the State
Foresaw it's happy Fate.
And now the Irish are asham'd
To see themselves in one Year tam'd:
75 So much one Man can do,
That does both act and know.
They can affirm his Praises best,
And have, though overcome, confest
How good he is, how just,
80 And fit for highest Trust:
Nor yet grown stiffer with Command,
But still in the Republick's hand:
How fit he is to sway
That can so well obey.
85 He to the Commons Feet presents
A Kingdome, for his first years rents:
And, what he may, forbears
His Fame to make it theirs:
And has his Sword and Spoyls ungirt,
90 To lay them at the Publick's skirt.
So when the Falcon high
Falls heavy from the Sky,
She, having kill'd, no more does search,
But on the next green Bow to pearch;

69 *A bleeding Head:* Holland's *Pliny,* Book XXVIII, ch. 2, recounts the finding of a man's head, when the foundations were dug for the temple on the Capitol.

74 *To see themselves in one Year tam'd:* Cromwell's subduing of Ireland took only nine months, from August 1649.

82 *But still in the Republick's hand:* accepting the principle of democratic rule.

95   Where, when he first does lure,
      The Falckner has her sure.
      What may not then our Isle presume
      While Victory his Crest does plume!
      What may not others fear
100   If thus he crown each Year!
      A Caesar he ere long to Gaul,
      To Italy an Hannibal,
        And to all States not free
        Shall Clymacterick be.
105   The Pict no shelter now shall find
      Within his party-colour'd Mind;
        But from this Valour sad
        Shrink underneath the Plad:
      Happy if in the tufted brake
110   The English Hunter him mistake;
        Nor lay his Hounds in near
        The Caledonian Deer.
      But thou the Wars and Fortunes Son
      March indefatigably on:
115   And for the last effect
        Still keep thy Sword erect;
      Besides the force it has to fright
      The Spirits of the shady Night,
        The same Arts that did gain
120   A Pow'r must it maintain.

104 *Clymacterick:* critical or fatal event or period.

106 *his party-colour'd Mind:* The ancient Picts coloured their bodies, and the seventeenth-century Scots were party-conscious. The pun is a subtle one.

107 *sad:* steadfast.

107-12 Marvell's wit at the expense of the Scots is near the facetious.

118 *The Spirits of the shady Night:* the powers of evil, which the cross made by the sword's hilt would dispel.

6. HYMNS

"HYMNOS" was a choral invocation sung round the altar to the Greek gods. It took the form of an ode accompanied by the *cithara*, a stringed instrument resembling the modern guitar. Hymns were of earlier Oriental origin than the Hellenic poems, being sung at religious festivals in ancient Egypt, Assyria, China and India; but they were not taken over by Roman poets until the Christian period, with individual exceptions in the case of Catullus and Horace. St. Augustine adapted the Hebrew psalmody to Christian needs, and called the hymn a *canticum*, which included praises in rhythmical prose to the Deity or saints. St. Hilary, St. Ambrose and St. Benedict introduced the hymnody into the western Church services from the eastern, and hymns were regularly sung at the canonical hours in the Catholic Church. Luther wrote hymns for the Protestant Church and instituted the "house choir" of friends to adapt traditional melodies. The earliest hymnody of Britain was the work of Thomas Sternhold, of the household of Henry VIII, and John Hopkins, a Suffolk clergyman. King James I translated thirty-one of the psalms, to which his adviser, Sir William Alexander, added others, approved by a committee of archbishops of England, Scotland and Ireland. They were published by the Oxford University Press in 1631. George Wither, Milton and Dryden wrote, or translated hymns; but the most fertile period of innovations and additions came in the eighteenth century from Isaac Watts, Charles Wesley, John Newton and William Cowper. Hymns were now regarded as "acts of devotion", and were selected by the religious denominations for other than literary reasons. Thus the hymn-writers of the eighteenth and nineteenth centuries virtually became anonymous adapters of lessons from the Bible to augment the sermons.

In this selection, only the first two poems recall the pagan origins of the hymn.

Sir Walter Raleigh

PRAISD BE DIANAS FAIRE
AND HARMLES LIGHT

THE poem appears in *The Phoenix Nest* (1593) which contains a number of anonymous pieces. In *Englands Helicon* (1600) it appears with the subscription Ignoto (Anonymous) over the initials S.W.R. The hymn bears some resemblance to lines 11-18 of Raleigh's *Cynthia*, Book XII, and was first ascribed to him by Francis Davison in MS. Harley 280. Diana (the Moon) and Cynthia both represent Queen Elizabeth, with whom Raleigh was genuinely or diplomatically in love, before his disgrace in 1589. It was generally held that his praise of the Monarch in *Cynthia*, which he did not venture to publish, restored him to Elizabeth's favour. In a letter of 1592 to Lord Cecil, he wrote that he "was wount to behold her riding like Alexander, huntinge like Diana, walking like Venus, the gentle winde blowinge her faire heare about her pure cheekes like a nimph, sumetyme sittinge in the shade like a goddess, sumetyme playinge like Orpheus". Diana was a Roman deity of the woodlands, a virgin huntress, who was identified with the Greek Artemis, twin sister of Apollo. She was the goddess of chastity, though in pre-Hellenic times connected with the rites of fertility. Artemis was born on the island of Delos at the foot of Mount Cynthus, hence her other name Cynthia.

> Praisd be Dianas faire and harmles light,
> Praisd be the dewes, wherwith she moists the ground;
> Praisd be hir beames, the glorie of the night,
> Praisd be hir powre, by which all powres abound.
>
> 5 Praisd be hir Nimphs, with whom she decks the woods,
> Praisd be hir knights, in whom true honor lives,
> Praisd be that force, by which she moves the floods,
> Let that Diana shine, which all these gives.
>
> In heaven Queene she is among the spheares,
> 10 In ay she Mistres like makes all things pure,
> Eternitie in hir oft chaunge she beares,
> She beautie is, by hir the faire endure.
>
> Time weares hir not, she doth his chariot guide,
> Mortalitie belowe hir orbe is plaste,

1 *harmles light:* The light of the moon has not the fecundity of the sun. Diana was the goddess of Chastity. The likeness of Elizabeth to Diana, in her powers, is allegorical.

5 *Nimphs:* attendants.

10 *In ay:* The meaning of *ay* seems to be "everything". E. K. Chambers emended to *earth*, giving *ay(r)* as an alternative reading. Used as an adverb, *ay* generally meant "ever, always".

11 *Eternitie in hir oft chaunge she beares:* Even in her frequent changes (of mood or policy) she remains the symbol of constancy. The moon was traditionally regarded as inconstant in its influence.

13 *she doth his chariot guide:* She rules the day; the chariot being the symbol of Apollo's daily journey across the Heavens.

15   By hir the vertue of the starrs downe slide,
      In hir is vertues perfect image cast.

      A knowledge pure it is hir worth to kno,
      With Circes let them dwell that thinke not so.

15 *By hir the vertue of the starrs downe slide:* The stars were believed to control human destiny; but Diana overrules their influence.

18 *Circes:* Tasting of Circe's magic cup, the companions of Ulysses were turned into swine, until he restored them to human shape with the help of Hermes. Circe was, according to Homer, the daughter of Helios, the sun.

Ben Jonson

QUEENE AND HUNTRESSE, CHASTE AND FAIRE

THIS classic song to Diana, which anticipates the measured dignity of Milton's minor poems, is found in *Cynthia's Revels*, Act V, Scene 6, a satirical comedy sub-titled "The Fountain of Self-Love", performed 1600, published 1601.

      Queene and Huntresse, chaste and faire,
      Now the Sunne is laid to sleepe,
      Seated, in thy silver chaire,
      State in wonted manner keepe:
5   Hesperus intreats thy light,
          Goddesse, excellently bright.

      Earth, let not thy envious shade
      Dare it selfe to interpose,
      Cynthias shining orbe was made
10   Heaven to cleere, when day did close:
          Blesse us then with wished sight,
          Goddesse, excellently bright.

5 *Hesperus:* the name given to the planet *Venus,* but only when it appeared before the setting of the sun. If it appeared after sunset, it was called Lucifer or Phosphorus. Hesperus was the son of Japetus and brother of Atlas.

Lay thy bow of pearle apart,
And thy cristall-shining quiver;
15 Give unto the flying hart
Space to breathe, how short soever:
Thou, that mak'st a day of night,
Goddesse, excellently bright.

A HYMNE TO GOD THE FATHER

Under-Wood, published in the *Second Folio* of Ben Jonson (1640), opened
with three devotional poems, this hymn being the second. It consists of two
groups of three stanzas each, the first in each group being six lined, and the
two following five lined. Herrick wrote many stanzas with this simplicity
and short-verse rhythm in mind.

Heare mee, O God!
A broken heart
Is my best part:
Use still thy rod,
5   That I may prove
Therein, thy Love.

If thou hadst not
Beene sterne to mee,
But left me free,
10 I had forgot
My selfe and thee.

For, sin's so sweet,
As minds ill bent
Rarely repent,
15 Untill they meet
Their punishment.

Who more can crave
Then thou hast done?
That gav'st a Sonne,
20 To free a slave,
First made of nought;
With all since bought.

5 *prove:* learn by experience.   **22** *bought:* redeemed.

Sinne, Death, and Hell,
His glorious Name
25 Quite overcame,
Yet I rebell,
And slight the same.

But, I'le come in,
Before my losse
30 Me farther tosse,
As sure to win
Under his Crosse.

Robert Herrick

A THANKSGIVING TO GOD, FOR HIS HOUSE

HERRICK abounds in delicate poems of cottage economy, which have a harvest-festival piety of this kind. The shorter line in the couplet acts as a pleasant echo to the first.

Lord, Thou hast given me a cell
Wherein to dwell;
And little house, whose humble Roof
Is weather-proof;
5 Under the sparres of which I lie
Both soft, and drie;
Where Thou my chamber for to ward
Hast set a Guard
Of harmlesse thoughts, to watch and keep
10 Me, while I sleep.
Low is my porch, as is my Fate,
Both void of state;
And yet the threshold of my doore
Is worn by' the poore,

7-9 Suggested by Jonson's "Epode" (*The Forest*, XI. 7-8).
13-14 Suggested by *Ecclesiasticus*, vi, 36 and Martial, X. 10. 2.

15 Who thither come, and freely get
          Good words, or meat:
    Like as my Parlour, so my Hall
          And Kitchin's small:
    A little Butterie, and therein
20   A little Byn,
    Which keeps my little loafe of Bread
          Unchipt, unflead:
    Some brittle sticks of Thorne or Briar
          Make me a fire,
25 Close by whose living coale I sit,
          And glow like it.
    Lord, I confesse too, when I dine,
          The Pulse is Thine,
    And all those other Bits, that bee
30   There plac'd by Thee;
    The Worts, the Purslain, and the Messe
          Of Water-cresse,
    Which of Thy kindnesse Thou hast sent;
          And my content
35 Makes those, and my beloved Beet,
          To be more sweet.
    'Tis thou that crown'st my glittering Hearth
          With guiltlesse mirth;
    And giv'st me Wassaile Bowles to drink,
40   Spic'd to the brink.
    Lord, 'tis thy plenty-dropping hand,
          That soiles my land;
    And giv'st me, for my Bushell sowne,
          Twice ten for one:
45 Thou mak'st my teeming Hen to lay
          Her egg each day:

22 *unflead:* unspoilt, not nibbled by mice.

28 *The Pulse:* leguminous edible seeds, such as beans, peas and lentils.

31 *Worts:* general name for plants of the cabbage family.   *Purslain:* purslane, a pot-herb used for salads; from Latin *porcilaca* used by Pliny for *portulaca*, which belongs to the same genus.

42 *soiles:* fertilizes.

Besides my healthfull Ewes to beare
Me twins each yeare:
The while the conduits of my Kine
50   Run Creame, (for Wine.)
All these, and better Thou dost send
Me, to this end,
That I should render, for my part,
A thankfull heart;
55 Which, fir'd with incense, I resigne,
As wholly Thine;
But the acceptance, that must be,
My Christ, by Thee.

49 *conduits:* udders (a conceit).

Sidney Godolphin

LORD, WHEN THE WISE MEN CAME FROM FARR

THE beautiful simplicity and clarity of this hymn deserve to be better
known. Godolphin's theme is the equal acceptance, by God, of knowledge
and love. Both are sanctified by faith. The text is from Bodleian Library
MS. Malone 13.

Lord, when the wise men came from farr,
Led to thy Cradle by a Starr,
Then did the shepheards too rejoyce,
Instructed by thy Angels voyce:
5   Blest were the wisemen in their skill
And shepheards in their harmlesse will.

Wisemen in tracing Natures lawes
Ascend unto the highest Cause;
Shepheards with humble fearefulnesse
10 Walke safely, though their light be lesse:
Though wisemen better know the way
It seems noe honest heart can stray.

6 *will:* disposition, inclination, joy.
10 *lesse:* an emendation. The original reading was *life.*

Ther is no merrit in the wise
But love, (the shepheards sacrifice)
15　Wisemen all ways of knowledge past,
To th' shepheards wonder come at last:
To know, can only wonder breede,
And not to know, is wonders seede.

A wiseman at the Altar bowes
20　And offers up his studied vowes,
And is received; may not the teares,
Which spring too from a shepheards feares,
And sighs upon his fraylty spent,
Though not distinct, be eloquent?

25　'Tis true, the object sanctifies
All passions which within us rise,
But since noe creature comprehends
The cause of causes, end of ends,
Hee who himselfe vouchsafes to know
30　Best pleases his creator soe.

When then our sorrowes we applye
To our owne wantes and poverty,
When wee looke up in all distresse
And our owne misery confesse,
35　Sending both thankes and prayers above,
Then though we doe not know, we love.

Henry Vaughan

A WELSHMAN from Brecknockshire, Vaughan called himself the Silurist, because he came from the region of the Cymric tribe of Silures. He was the friend and relative of John Aubrey, his earliest biographer, and spent two years at Jesus College, Oxford; but left, without graduating, to study law in London. Finally he took up medicine as a profession, and practised it on his return to Wales at the commencement of the Civil War in 1642. As local poet, he became known as "The Swan of Usk", spending the remainder of his days at Newton on that river. Besides a medical treatise, he published between 1646 and 1657 several volumes of verse, including translations of

Ovid, Juvenal and Boethius. Two books of sacred poems appeared under the title *Silex Scintillans*, meaning "Flashing Flint-Stone". He explained the significance of this when he wrote: "Certaine Divine Raies breake out of the Soul in adversity, like sparks of fire out of the afflicted flint." He published in prose several works of religious meditation which explain the conversion caused by his afflictions. His sensitive appreciation of nature, and indirect influence upon the poet-philosopher of the "Immortality Ode" (though Wordsworth never actually read his poems) have been the subject of speculation.

LOVE, AND DISCIPLINE

PUBLISHED in 1650 in *Silex Scintillans, Sacred Poems and Private Ejaculations*. In the preface to the second edition, September 1654, Vaughan calls these poems hymns and explains that serious illness was the origin of his new-found piety. In his earlier poems he had been a fashionable wit and Platonist, with a taste for satire, following in the footsteps of Jonson and Donne. In the *Sacred Poems* his inspirations were the Bible and *The Temple* of George Herbert, whom he regarded as "the blessed man" of his age. Vaughan's colloquial simplicity does not conceal Neoplatonic mysticism, but emphasizes his sincere Christianity. The grouping of the triple rhymes is skilful; and, except in the third stanza, there is small trace in this poem of the metaphysical imagery he acquired from Herbert.

> Since in a land not barren stil
> (Because thou dost thy grace distil,)
> My lott is faln, Blest be thy will!
>
> And since these biting frosts but kil
> 5 Some tares in me which choke, or spil
> That seed thou sow'st, Blest be thy skil!
>
> Blest be thy Dew, and blest thy frost,
> And happy I to be so crost,
> And cur'd by Crosses at thy cost.
>
> 10 The Dew doth Cheer what is distrest,
> The frosts ill weeds nip, and molest,
> In both thou work'st unto the best.

2 *distil:* give forth in small drops.
5 *tares:* mediaeval name for weeds in a cornfield, of the vetch family. *spil:* destroy.

Thus while thy sev'ral mercies plot,
And work on me now cold, now hot,
15   The work goes on, and slacketh not,

For as thy hand the weather steers,
So thrive I best, 'twixt joyes, and tears,
And all the year have some grean Ears.

7. SONGS

SONGS, as Gilbert Highet has pointed out, have all "developed out of dance-rhythms and folk melodies". The secular songs of the Elizabethan Age are among the freshest and most joyous in the language. Every mood is expressed, spirited foreign models are tapped, and the range of metrical variety is unsurpassed. The strongest impacts were the shorter lyrics of Catullus, adapted from *The Greek Anthology*, and fifteenth-century English balladry. Simple word order and natural rhythms were the impulses of song from earliest times. Jonson argued against complicated stanzas that might compel the poet to say more than was necessary. Songs in plays effectively inhibited the lyric from becoming wordy.

The sonnet of Petrarch was the accepted mode for love-poetry in Europe; it was a Renaissance tradition that had to be broken. The music-loving Elizabethan lutenists took a hand in this, even before the advent of Jonson and Donne. Both poets disciplined love for expression in intellectual, rather than passionate, terms. Jonson shows the classical ideals of detachment and restraint as not incompatible with feeling. Though he is not a romantic lover, he does not suffer from the frigidity of Cowley. Feelings in classical poetry tend to be hinted, not paraded. Jonson rejected French and Italian styles, not because he did not understand the languages, but thought the logic-chopping of Neoplatonism affected. Jonson and Donne accepted their destiny as a hard fact, and mocked at the self-pitying extravagances of rejected Provençal love-poets.

Donne was a wit, not a distinguished poet in the Elizabethan sense; critics thought him wanting in versification and musical feeling. Conceits from science were suggested by his Italian reading in Petrarch, Marino and Dante, not by English philosophy. The novelty of his diction lies in the unstilted grammar, manipulated to get impassioned emphasis into the logic; new, too, is his functional use of imagery. Jonson's images were not wholly from classical mythology, but they tend to be emblematic and decorative.

In the following selection the love poems come first, then songs on the vicissitudes of life, its brevity, mutability, joy and sadness.

Thomas Wyatt

MY LUTE AWAKE!

THIS is a transitional poem, written in the spirit of the mediaeval complaint, a relic of the Provençal Courts of Love. The poet's plaint to his lute is to sing the lover's final word to a cruel mistress, a theme that had become monotonously self-pitying before Wyatt handled it. It cloys even in a masterpiece like *The Knight's Tale*; but it is a poetic convention that has to be accepted, along with Wyatt's French and Italian stanza forms. He used his emotions as impersonal material for art; we cannot therefore judge the extent of the poet's sincerity. Rarely does he describe, like Spenser, the physical attributes of his beloved or her responses; but he is voluble on her pride and fickleness. Wyatt's debt to the Roman poets, whom he knew, is seen mainly in his satires on life at Court, in the spirit of Horace, Persius and Juvenal. His English style in all his poems is plain and workmanlike, like that of George Gascoigne; but he is a more sensitive poet. What is surprising is Wyatt's ear for rhythm, at a time when versification was halting in the placing of its accents.

My lute awake! perfourme the last
Labor that thou and I shall wast,
    And end that I have now begon;
For when this song is sung and past,
5   My lute be still, for I have done.

As to be herd where ere is none,
As lede to grave in marbill stone,
    My song may perse her hert as sone;
Should we then sigh, or syng, or mone?
10   No, no, my lute, for I have done.

The Rokkes do not so cruelly
Repulse the waves continuelly,
    As she my suyte and affection,
So that I ame past remedy:
15   Whereby my lute and I have done.

6 *ere:* ear.   **7** *lede:* lead.

Prowd of the spoyll that thou hast gott
Of simple hertes thorough loves shot,
By whome, unkynd, thou hast theim wone,
Thinck not he haith his bow forgot,
20   All tho my lute and I have done.

Vengeaunce shall fall on thy disdain,
That makest but game on ernest pain;
Thinck not alone under the sonne
Unquyt to cause thy lovers plain,
25   All tho my lute and I have done.

Perchaunce the lye wethered and old,
The wynter nyghtes that are so cold,
Playnyng in vain unto the mone;
Thy wisshes then dare not be told;
30   Care then who lyst, for I have done.

And then may chaunce the to repent
The tyme that thou hast lost and spent
To cause thy lovers sigh and swoune;
Then shalt thou knowe beaultie but lent,
35   And wisshe and want as I have done.

Now cesse, my lute, this is the last
Labour that thou and I shall wast,
And ended is that we begon;
Now is this song boeth sung and past:
40   My lute be still, for I have done.

18 *whome:* the antecedent is "love", i.e. Cupid.   23 *sonne:* sun.
24 *Unquyt:* unrequited.   26 *the lye wethered:* thou mayest lie withered.
28 *mone:* moon.   33 *swoune:* fit of faintness.   34 *beaultie:* beauty.

AND WYLT THOW LEVE ME THUS?

THIS complaint, with its haunting repetition in the first line of each stanza,
followed by a rhyming triplet and a two-lined refrain, is one of the most
perfect of Wyatt's lyrics, well adapted to musical accompaniment. The
smoothness of the rhythm is due largely to the management of the liquid

and nasal consonants, the use of alliteration and assonance, and the occasional
Anglo-Saxon amplification, such as *greffe and grame* (which mean the same
thing), and *payn nor smart*. The last stanza has a Gallic quality, in its accentua-
tion of *Pyttye* and the use of *Helas*.

> And wylt thow leve me thus?
> Say nay, say nay, ffor shame,
> To save the from the Blame
> Of all my greffe and grame;
> 5   And wylt thow leve me thus?
>   Say nay, Say nay!
>
> And wylt thow leve me thus,
> That hathe lovyd the so long,
> In welthe and woo among?
> 10 And ys thy hart so strong
> As for to leve me thus?
>   Say nay, Say nay!
>
> And wylt thow leve me thus,
> That hathe gevyn the my hart,
> 15 Never for to Depart,
> Nother for payn nor smart;
> And wylt thow leve me thus?
>   Say nay, Say nay!
>
> And wylt thow leve me thus
> 20 And have nomore Pyttye
> Of hym that lovythe the?
> Helas thy cruellte!
> And wylt thow leve me thus?
>   Say nay, Say nay!

4 *grame:* sorrow.   9 *welthe:* prosperity.

16 *Nother:* neither.   *smart:* sharp pain, often used for mental suffering.

20 *Pyttye:* The stress is on the second syllable.

22 *Helas:* French form of *alas*.

Anonymous

A PROPER NEW DITY: INTITULED FIE UPON LOVE AND AL HIS LAWES

OCCASIONALLY the complaint has a tone of reproving bitterness, mildly satirical, which is amusing in its rejection of love as a non-fatal disease of the mind. Hence the title of the book from which this poem is taken, *A Handful of Pleasant Delights* (1584), containing flyting poems of Clement Robinson and others, probably first published in 1566. The text is from the edition of Hyder E. Rollins (Harvard University Press, 1924), based on the unique copy in the British Museum. Rollins describes the poems as "broadside ballads", most of them being composed for singing to existing popular tunes. The book was known to Shakespeare, since there are echoes of it in Ophelia's song in *Hamlet*, Act IV, Scene 5, and elsewhere in the plays. Edward Arber reprinted, but modernized, the full text of the book in 1878. Thomas Park in 1815 praised the poems for their "apposite metaphor, sarcastic sportiveness, ingenious illustration, and moral influence". The ballads, among which is "Greensleeves", are Elizabethan popular poetry at its best. The reason for inclusion of this one among English classical poems is their plain and unromantic style; Petrarchism is not mocked, but is not seriously considered. The disappointments of love are treated with the cold common sense afterwards assumed by the sophisticated Cavalier poet, Sir John Suckling. Practically nothing is known of the author-collector, Clement Robinson.

> Such bitter fruict thy love doth yeelde,
> Such broken sleepes, such hope unsure,
> Thy call so oft hath me beguilde,
> That I unneth can well indure:
> 5   But crie (alas) as I have cause,
> Fie upon Love and all his Lawes.
>
> Like Piramus, I sigh and grone,
> Whom Stonie wals, keept from his love,

4 *unneth:* not easily.

7 *Piramus:* The story of Pyramus and Thisbe, Babylonian lovers thwarted by their parents, is told in the Fourth Book of Ovid's *Metamorphoses*. They were only able to converse through a cranny in the wall of their adjoining homes. Both eventually committed suicide.

And as the wofull Palemon,
10   A thousand stormes, for thee I proove,
     Yet thou a cruell Tigers whelpe,
     All slaiest the hart, whom thou maist help.

     A craggie Rocke, thy Cradle was,
     And Tigers milke sure was thy foode,
15   Whereby Dame Nature broought to passe,
     That like the Nurse should be thy moode:
     Wild and unkinde, cruell and fell,
     to rent the hart that loves thee well.

     The Crocadile with fained teares,
20   The Fisher not so oft beguiles:
     As thou hast luld my simple eares,
     To here sweet words, full fraught w' wiles,
     that I may say, as I doo proove,
     Wo worth the time, I gan to love.

25   Sith thou hast vowd to worke my wrack,
     And hast no will my wealth to way:
     Farewell unkinde, I will keepe backe,
     Such toyes as may my helth decay:
     and still will cry as I have cause.
30   Fie upon Love and all his lawes

9 *Palemon:* the hero in Chaucer's *The Knight's Tale.*
10 *proove:* experience.
13-14 A reference to Vergil's *Æneid*, IV, 365-7.
16 *the Nurse:* the tigress that suckles the human child.
17 *fell:* savage, ruthless.
18 *rent:* rend.
19 *The Crocadile with fained teares:* According to fable the crocodile weeps either to attract its human prey, or from pleasure while devouring him.
22 *w':* with.
25 *wrack:* ruin.
26 *my wealth to way:* to consider my welfare.
28 *toyes:* trifling annoyances.

Thomas Campion

THE lutenist, Campion, was one of a group of famous song-composers that brought scholars from abroad to study music. He actually wrote a technical book on counterpoint. He seems to have been educated at Cambridge, though he took no degree there, probably because he was a Catholic. Later he studied law at Grays Inn, and then practised medicine. From his pen there flowed not only two books of excellent Latin verse epigrams, but five books of airs and lyrics (published 1601-17), as well as four masques, controversial prose and a treatise, *Observations on the Art of English Poesy* (1602). At the age of twenty-eight he was hailed as "Sweet Master Campion", although he had, as yet, published only his *Latin Epigrams* (1594), many of which are on his literary contemporaries. From the suddenness of his death and verbal will, he is thought to have died of the plague.

The classical grace and verbal economy of Campion's lyrics is the fruit of long study of Catullus and Horace. His range of metrical experiments is immense, and the frequent changes of rhythm are often surprising, except to those who see the reasons in the influence of classical measures or musical accompaniments. He is thought to have fitted words to music, which he composed first; this may explain the often fluid placing of his caesuras. In his address to the reader (*Book of Airs*, 1601) he writes: "The lyric poets among the Greeks and Latins were first inventors of airs, tying themselves strictly to the number and value of their syllables: of which sort, you shall find here, only one song in Sapphic verse; the rest are after the fashion of the time. . . . The subject of them is, for the most part, amorous . . . we ought to maintain, as well in notes as in action, a manly carriage; gracing no word, but that which is eminent and emphatical."

The three poems selected are from the first and third *Book of Airs*, the text being from the *Works*, ed. Percival Vivian (Clarendon Press).

AND WOULD YOU SEE MY MISTRIS FACE?

THE poem appears in *A Book of Airs* and also in Francis Davison's *Poetical Rhapsody* (1602). Most of Campion's compositions were in private circulation.

> And would you see my Mistris face?
>   It is a flowrie garden place,
> Where knots of beauties have such grace
>   That all is worke and nowhere space.

3 *knots*: flower-beds of intricate design.

5   It is a sweete delicious morne,
    Where day is breeding, never borne,
    It is a Meadow yet unshorne,
    Whome thousand flowers do adorne.

    It is the heavens bright reflexe,
10   Weake eies to dazle and to vexe,
    It is th' Idæa of her sexe,
    Envie of whome doth world perplexe.

    It is a face of death that smiles,
    Pleasing, though it killes the whiles,
15 Where death and love in pretie wiles
    Each other mutuallie beguiles.

    It is faire beauties freshest youth,
    It is the fain'd Eliziums truth:
    The spring that winter'd harts renu'th;
20   And this is that my soule pursu'th.

8 *Whome: who* and *which* were used interchangeably for persons and things.

11 *Idæa:* the perfect form or pattern conceived by the Supreme Mind.

14 Change from iambic to trochaic rhythm, not merely in initial foot.

18 *the fain'd Elizium:* Elysium, the pretended western country in Homer to which favoured heroes passed happily, without dying; a temperate land by the sea, without frost or rain, ruled over by Rhadamanthus. Among Latin poets Elysium was the abode of blessed shades after death, situated in the lower world.

19 *winter'd harts:* A recollection of *Psalm* xlii, 1. Winter is the dry season in many parts of the earth. There is also a pun intended, implying "dreary hearts".

IF LOVE LOVES TRUTH, THEN WOMEN DOE NOT LOVE

THIS poem was in 1652 also set to music by Henry Lawes, Milton's musical collaborator. Each stanza consists of a quatrain rounded off with a couplet, the last being an example of Campion's paradoxical wit, much favoured as an ending by the Cavalier poets.

If Love loves truth, then women doe not love;
Their passions all are but dissembled shewes;
Now kinde and free of favour if they prove,
Their kindnes straight a tempest overthrowes.
5   Then as a Sea-man the poore lover fares;
     The storme drownes him ere hee can drowne his cares.

But why accuse I women that deceive?
Blame then the Foxes for their subtile wile:
They first from Nature did their craft receive:
10 It is a womans nature to beguile.
     Yet some, I grant, in loving stedfast grow;
     But such by use are made, not nature, so.

O why had Nature power at once to frame
Deceit and Beauty, traitors both to Love?
15 O would Deceit had dyed when Beauty came
With her divinenesse ev'ry heart to move!
     Yet doe we rather wish, what ere befall,
     To have fayre women false then none at all.

Ben Jonson

IF I FREELY MAY DISCOVER

THE song appears in *Poetaster*, II. 2, performed in 1601. The stanzas are sung by different characters. Even in love, Jonson advocates, with Horace, the avoidance of extremes; but his ideal of love invariably expresses the male point of view. There is a hint for the poem in Martial, I. 57.

If I feely may discover,
What would please me in my lover:
     I would have her faire, and wittie,
     Savouring more of court, then cittie;
5   A little proud, but full of pittie:
Light and humorous in her toying
Oft building hopes, and soone destroying,
Long, but sweet in the enjoying,
     Neither too easie, nor too hard:
10 All extreames I would have bard.

Shee should be allowed her passions,
So they were but us'd as fashions;
  Sometimes froward, and then frowning,
  Sometimes sickish, and then swowning,
15 Every fit, with change, still crowning.
Purely Jelous, I would have her,
Then onely constant when I crave her.
'Tis a vertue should not save her.
Thus, nor her delicates would cloy me,
20 Neither her peevishnesse annoy me.

15 *fit:* mood.
16 *Purely:* entirely.   *Jelous:* covetous of love, amorous.
19 *delicates:* secret charms.

Thomas Carew

ASKE ME NO MORE WHERE JOVE BESTOWES

THIS song is found in a number of manuscripts, in which the stanzas are differently arranged or expanded. It was translated into Latin by Arthur Johnston in 1642 and often parodied, answered or imitated, not only in the seventeenth century, but by Tennyson in *The Princess*, Part VI. The poem is metaphysical in its conceits; but the handling of the verse and allusions to Greek science and mythology are classical. The fourth stanza illustrates the contention of George Williamson in *The Donne Tradition* that "Jonson has intervened to make Carew's image less difficult and more commonplace" (p. 206).

Aske me no more where Jove bestowes,
When June is past, the fading rose:
For in your beauties orient deepe,
These flowers as in their causes, sleepe.

4 *as in their causes:* The idea of this conceit is derived from Aristotle's *Physics*, II. 3, in which four causes are distinguished; the material, the formal, the efficient and the purposive. R. Dunlap in his edition of the *Poems* sees this conceit as illustrating a formal causation, the sleep of the flowers being the result of the beauty of the lady. The meaning of *orient deepe* is obscure.

5 Aske me no more whether doth stray,
   The golden Atomes of the day:
   For in pure love heaven did prepare
   Those powders to inrich your haire.

   Aske me no more whether doth hast,
10 The Nightingale when May is past:
   For in your sweet dividing throat,
   She winters and keepes warme her note.

   Aske me no more where those starres light,
   That downewards fall in dead of night:
15 For in your eyes they sit, and there,
   Fixed become as in their sphere.

   Aske me no more if East or West,
   The Phenix builds her spicy nest:
   For unto you at last shee flies,
20 And in your fragrant bosome dyes.

5 *whether:* whither.

6 *Atomes:* minute particles or motes of dust by which the sun's rays were supposed to be conveyed to the earth. Atoms as ultimate particles of matter were first conceived by Leucippus and Democritus.

11 *dividing:* melodiously quavering or trilling, as in a descant.

13 *light:* alight.

16 *as in their sphere:* In the Ptolemaic cosmology, each sphere was a concentric, hollow, transparent sphere revolving round the earth, and taking with it its appropriate planet.

18 *The Phenix builds her spicy nest:* The legendary bird was said to nest on a heap of burning aromatic wood.

Edmund Waller

TO CHLORIS UPPON A FAVOUR RECEAVED

THIS slight, but typical, Cavalier lyric, appears in Waller's first volume of 1645. Dr. Johnson says of the poet: "He seems neither to have had a mind much elevated by nature, nor amplified by learning. His thoughts are such as a liberal conversation and large acquaintance with life would easily supply." This is true of Waller's attitude to women. One secret of his smooth versification is his intricate, but unobtrusive, use of alliteration—in this poem mainly on the fricatives *f* and *s*. A long simile in the final stanza is a poetic device he much favoured.

> Chloris! since first our calm of peace
>   Was frighted hence, this good we find,
> Your favours with your fears increase,
>   And growing mischiefs make you kind.
>
> 5 So the fair tree, which still preserves
>   Her fruit and state, while no wind blows;
> In storms from that uprightness swerves,
>   And the glad earth about her strows
>   With treasure, from her yielding boughs.

GO, LOVELY ROSE!

THIS, the most perfect, and deservedly the best known of Waller's lyrics, is seldom omitted from an anthology. It captures the cynical indifference of dalliance in love characteristic of Cavalier song-writers. Pope imitated the poem in the first of his *Pastorals*, "Spring"; but the implied simile in the first stanza, sustained throughout the poem, is a commonplace of sixteenth- and seventeenth-century poetry. It occurs in Chaucer, the *Colloquies* of Erasmus and Spenser's *Faerie Queene*, and seems to derive from Catullus and Ausonius. Always, Waller manages this five-lined stanza, using short first and third lines, with artistry, especially in the modulation of vowels and consonants.

> Go, lovely rose!
> Tell her, that wastes her time and me,
>   That now she knows,
>   When I resemble her to thee,
> 5 How sweet, and fair, she seems to be.
>
> Tell her that's young,
> And shuns to have her graces spy'd,
>   That hadst thou sprung
>   In deserts, where no men abide,
> 10 Thou must have uncommended dy'd.

7 *her graces spy'd:* her beauty looked upon.

Small is the worth
Of beauty, from the light retir'd:
Bid her come forth,
Suffer herself to be desir'd,
15   And not blush so to be admir'd.

Then die! that she
The common fate of all things rare
May read in thee:
How small a part of time they share
20   That are so wondrous sweet and fair!

Thomas Stanley

STANLEY was an East Anglian gentleman of means, who was privately tutored by William Fairfax, until at thirteen he entered Pembroke College, Cambridge, only to move within a year to the University of Oxford. He was one of the Royalists who remained in England during the Civil War, leading the life of a literary recluse. An excellent classical scholar, he wrote a *History of Philosophy* (1655), edited Aeschylus (1663) and translated Anacreon (ed. Bullen, 1893). Most of his poetry is translation from the classics or the leading Italian, French and Spanish poets. Consequently his original poems in English, privately published in 1647 and 1651 and augmented from various sources by Sir Egerton Brydges in 1814, have been neglected. Some uncollected poems had also appeared in Gamble's *Airs and Dialogues* (1656); others were set to music in 1657 by Professor John Wilson of Oxford.

LOVE'S HERETIC

LIVING in London, Stanley was acquainted with most of the Cavalier poets. This antithetical poem resembles, in tone, some of the rationalizations of Richard Lovelace or Sir John Suckling. There is no reason to suspect gallantry in Stanley's life; for he married young and begot a large family in circumstances of uneventful domestic peace. He sought no more than the scholarly accomplishments of a humanist; and the only laxity may be observed in his versification. In lines 2-4 of the opening stanza, limping trochaics are varied with trisyllabic rising rhythms. Uncertain accentuation troubles the reader throughout, and the proximity of words like *active* and *captive* is unpleasing to the ear. He translated too much from other tongues to be conscious of the natural harmonies of English speech. The "starlight of her eyes" (line 53) is an odd premonition of the modern popular ballad.

He whose active thoughts disdain
    To be captive to one foe,
And would break his single chain,
    Or else more would undergo;
5 Let him learn the art of me,
    By new bondage to be free!

What tyrannic mistress dare
    To one beauty love confine,
Who, unbounded as the air,
10   All may court but none decline?
Why should we the heart deny
    As many objects as the eye?

Wheresoe'er I turn or move,
    A new passion doth detain me:
15 Those kind beauties that do love,
    Or those proud ones that disdain me;
This frown melts, and that smile burns me;
This to tears, that ashes turns me.

Soft fresh Virgins, not full blown,
20   With their youthful sweetness take me;
Sober Matrons, that have known
    Long since what these prove, awake me;
Here staid coldness I admire;
There the lively active fire.

25 She that doth by skill dispense
    Every favour she bestows,
Or the harmless innocence,
    Which nor court nor city knows,
Both alike my soul enflame,
30 That wild Beauty, and this tame.

She that wisely can adorn
    Nature with the wealth of Art,
Or whose rural sweets do scorn
    Borrow'd helps to take a heart,
35 The vain care of that's my pleasure,
Poverty of this my treasure.

Both the wanton and the coy,
    Me with equal pleasures move;
She whom I by force enjoy,
40   Or who forceth me to love:
This, because she'll not confess,
That not hide, her happiness.

She whose loosely flowing hair,
    Scatter'd like the beams o'th'morn,
45 Playing with the sportive air,
    Hides the sweets it doth adorn,
Captive in that net restrains me,
In those golden fetters chains me.

Nor doth she with power less bright
50   My divided heart invade,
Whose soft tresses spread like night
    O'er her shoulders a black shade;
For the starlight of her eyes
Brighter shines through those dark skies.

55 Black, or fair, or tall, or low,
    I alike with all can sport;
The bold sprightly Thais woo,
    Or the frozen Vestal court;
Every Beauty takes my mind,
60 Tied to all, to none confin'd.

57 *Thais:* a courtesan of Athens who accompanied Alexander on his Asian conquests.

58 *Vestal:* Six Vestal virgins, or priestesses, kept alive the flame on the altar of Vesta, goddess of the Roman hearth, and the most sacred symbol of their pagan religion. If their chastity was violated, they were buried alive.

Andrew Marvell

THE MOWER'S SONG

MARVELL wrote four Mower poems, and three stanzas in "Appleton House" appraise the Arcadian joys of the craft of the scythe, which derive from classical pastoral poetry. But Marvell's perceptions of rural pleasures are always at first hand. Miss V. Sackville-West in *Andrew Marvell* (1929) wrote: "Variations of light and shade were to him a perpetual delight; but of all colours it was green that enchanted him most; the world of his mind was a glaucous world, as though he lived in a coppice, stippled with sunlight and alive with moving shadows." This is one of only three poems in which Marvell uses anisometrical stanzas (i.e. containing lines of unequal length), here employing an alexandrine for the refrain, after five octosyllabic lines. In the stanza of the "Horatian Ode" he had been anticipated by Richard Fanshawe (see Pierre Legouis, *Andrew Marvell*, pp. 79-87).

> My Mind was once the true survey
> Of all these Medows fresh and gay;
> And in the greenness of the Grass
> Did see its Hopes as in a Glass;
> 5   When Juliana came, and She
> What I do to the Grass, does to my Thoughts and Me.
>
> But these, while I with Sorrow pine,
> Grew more luxuriant still and fine;
> That not one Blade of Grass you spy'd,
> 10 But had a Flower on either side;
> When Juliana came, and She
> What I do to the Grass, does to my Thoughts and Me.
>
> Unthankful Medows, could you so
> A fellowship so true forego,
> 15 And in your gawdy May-games meet,
> While I lay trodden under feet?
> When Juliana came, and She
> What I do to the Grass, does to my Thoughts and Me.

5 *Juliana:* the young shepherdess lover addressed in the other pastorals, "Damon the Mower" and "The Mower to the Glo-Worms".

7 *these:* i.e. *Medows* in the previous stanza.

But what you in compassion ought,
20   Shall now by my Revenge be wrought:
And Flow'rs, and Grass, and I and all,
Will in one common Ruine fall.
For Juliana comes, and She
   What I do to the Grass, does to my Thoughts and Me.

25   And thus, ye Meadows, which have been
Companions of my thoughts more green
Shall now the Heraldry become
With which I shall adorn my Tomb;
For Juliana comes, and She
30   What I do to the Grass, does to my Thoughts and Me.

Thomas Campion

WHETHER MEN DOE LAUGH OR WEEPE

THE song is in falling or trochaic rhythm throughout. The tone is cynical.

Whether men doe laugh or weepe,
Whether they doe wake or sleepe,
Whether they die yoong or olde,
Whether they feele heate or colde;
5   There is, underneath the sunne,
Nothing in true earnest done.

All our pride is but a jest;
None are worst, and none are best;
Griefe, and joy, and hope, and feare,
10   Play their Pageants every where:
Vaine opinion all doth sway,
And the world is but a play.

Powers above in cloudes doe sit,
Mocking our poore apish wit;
15   That so lamely, with such state,
Their high glorie imitate:
No ill can be felt but paine,
And that happie men disdaine.

Ben Jonson

SLOW, SLOW, FRESH FOUNT, KEEPE TIME WITH MY SALT TEARES

THIS song is given to Echo in *Cynthia's Revels*, I. 2 (performed 1600). It was set to music as a canzonet for three voices by Henry Youll in 1608. The story of Echo's love for Narcissus is told in Ovid's *Metamorphoses*, Book III; her grief at unrequited love is suggested in the solemn movement of the verse.

Slow, slow, fresh fount, keepe time with my salt teares;
Yet slower, yet, ô faintly gentle springs:
List to the heavy part the musique beares,
　　Woe weepes out her division, when shee sings.
5　　　Droupe hearbs, and flowers,
　　　Fall grief in showers;
　　Our beauties are not ours:
　　　　O, I could still
(Like melting snow upon some craggie hill,)
10　　drop, drop, drop, drop,
Since natures pride is, now, a wither'd Daffodill.

4 *division:* in music, a run or variation of short notes to replace a succession of long notes in plain song—very like a descant.

STILL TO BE NEAT, STILL TO BE DREST

THIS song, set to music after the Restoration by Henry Lawes, is from *The Silent Woman*, I. 1 (performed 1609). The last two couplets gave a hint to Herrick for his "Delight in Disorder". Jonson himself may have owed the idea to Ovid, *Amores*, I. 14. 21.

Still to be neat, still to be drest,
As you were going to a feast;
Still to be pou'dred, still perfum'd:
Lady, it is to be presum'd,
5　Though arts hid causes are not found,
All is not sweet, all is not sound.

2 *as:* as if.

E

Give me a looke, give me a face,
That makes simplicitie a grace;
Robes loosely flowing, haire as free:
10   Such sweet neglect more taketh me,
Then all th'adulteries of art.
They strike mine eyes, but not my heart.

Robert Herrick

TO THE VIRGINS, TO MAKE MUCH OF TIME

IN Burton's *Anatomy of Melancholy*, Partition III, Section IV, Member II, Subsection I, occurs this passage: "let us crowne our selves with rose buds before they are withered, etc. *Vivamus, mea Lesbia, atque amemus.*" Herrick seems to have had this passage, and others in Burton, in mind, not only in this poem, but in the final stanza of "Corinna's going a-Maying". The idea of *Carpe diem* is as old as Anacreon and Catullus, and is also found in *The Wisdom of Solomon*. Spenser in the *Faerie Queene*, II, 12. 75 (6-9) has "Gather therefore the Rose, whilest yet is time". Lines 3 and 4 of the first stanza are from Catullus 42 (39-48); the third stanza is prompted by Ovid's *Ars Amatoria*, III (65-6); and lines 13 and 14 in the last stanza look back to Seneca's *Phaedra* (speech of Hippolytus) 446-51. Herrick has, in his apparently spontaneous way, expressed a hackneyed theme with delightful simplicity.

Gather ye Rose-buds while ye may,
   Old Time is still a flying:
And this same flower that smiles to day,
   To morrow will be dying.

5   The glorious Lamp of Heaven, the Sun,
   The higher he's a getting;
The sooner will his Race be run,
   And neerer he's to Setting.

That Age is best, which is the first,
10   When Youth and Blood are warmer;
But being spent, the worse, and worst
   Times, still succeed the former.

5 *The glorious Lamp of Heaven*: suggested by Fairfax's translation of Tasso's *Jerusalem Delivered*, VII. 116. 1—a popular metaphor for the sun in Elizabeth and Jacobean literature.

Then be not coy, but use your time;
And while ye may, goe marry:
15   For having lost but once your prime,
You may for ever tarry.

TO BLOSSOMS

THE theme of mutability and the brevity of life, as witnessed in nature, is a
favourite of Herrick's and of classical poets like Jonson, whose stanza of the
Lucius Cary ode ("It is not growing like a tree") has the moral force of the
last stanza of this poem. Herrick's mastery of the more superficial arts of
versification, such as alliteration, is similar to Waller's.

Faire pledges of a fruitfull Tree,
Why do yee fall so fast?
Your date is not so past;
But you may stay yet here a while,
5   To blush and gently smile;
And go at last.

What, were yee borne to be
An houre or half's delight;
And so to bid goodnight?
10   'Twas pitie Nature brought yee forth
Meerly to shew your worth,
And lose you quite.

But you are lovely Leaves, where we
May read how soon things have
15   Their end, though ne'r so brave:
And after they have shown their pride,
Like you a while: They glide
Into the Grave.

3 *date:* time.
13 *Leaves:* petals.
15 *brave:* attractive-looking.

John Milton

ON MAY MORNING

THIS poem appeared in the edition of 1645. Though the ten lines are in couplets, half of them are five-footers, the rest four-footers in the style of "L'Allegro". The musical quality of Milton's verse is already apparent, the rhythm inevitably suggesting the correct modulation. In the fineness of his ear, Milton is nearer to Greek than to Latin lyrists.

> Now the bright morning Star, Dayes harbinger,
> Comes dancing from the East, and leads with her
> The Flowry May, who from her green lap throws
> The yellow Cowslip, and the pale Primrose.
> 5   Hail bounteous May that dost inspire
> Mirth and youth, and warm desire,
> Woods and Groves, are of thy dressing,
> Hill and Dale, doth boast thy blessing.
> Thus we salute thee with our early Song,
> 10   And welcom thee, and wish thee long.

1 *the bright morning Star:* usually the planet Venus; but because it appears before sunrise it is sometimes called *Lucifer* (light-bearer).

Andrew Marvell

THE MOWER TO THE GLO-WORMS

MARVELL'S style is invariably classic in its firmness and logical clarity. As Pierre Legouis remarks, "He writes as a contemporary gentleman talked: no Spenserian archaisms, not many Latinisms . . . very few of those special terms the Renaissance had borrowed so widely from the technical vocabularies" (*Andrew Marvell*, p. 66). The charming use of "courteous" for the glow-worms, personified in the poem as "living Lamps", is typical of Marvell's unobscure nature-mysticism.

> Ye living Lamps, by whose dear light
> The Nightingale does sit so late,
> And studying all the Summer-night,
> Her matchless Songs does meditate;

5   Ye Country Comets, that portend
     No War, nor Princes funeral,
     Shining unto no higher end
     Then to presage the Grasses fall;

     Ye Glo-worms, whose officious Flame
10   To wandring Mowers shows the way,
     That in the Night have lost their aim,
     And after foolish Fires do stray;

     Your courteous Lights in vain you wast,
     Since Juliana here is come,
15   For She my Mind hath so displac'd
     That I shall never find my home.

5 *Country Comets:* It should be noted that the first line of each stanza contains a metaphor, metaphysical in idea, and neatly sustained in the other three lines. The tone in this stanza is one of harmless hyperbole.

8 *the Grasses fall:* referring to the stroke of the mower's scythe.

9 *officious:* The word is used with the old meaning of "eager to serve", not "meddlesome" or "unduly forward".

12 *foolish Fires:* The reference is to *ignis fatuus*, the Will-o'-the-wisp.

14 *Juliana:* the Mower's shepherdess lover.

15 *displac'd:* disturbed.

8. SONNETS

THE form of the sonnet, in Italian, French and English, was as varied as the uses of the epigrammatic short poem in Greek and Roman times. The rhyming structure of the Petrarchan sonnet was modified in England, especially by Surrey, who preferred the pattern eventually perfected by Shakespeare, three cumulating quatrains, resolved by an epigrammatic couplet. Fourteen-lined tributes to friends were often written as epigrams of seven couplets, for example by Ben Jonson in his eulogy of William Camden. According to Douglas Bush, Jonson "see(s) and think(s) and feel(s) in terms of the epigram"; he never wanted to be a Neoplatonist or sonneteer. Milton was the first to conceive the possibility of Horatian sonnets, like the Roman poet's shorter gratulatory odes. The three published in this selection illustrate the uses to which the sonnet could be put by poets who were judicial in tone and controlled in feeling. But the English form, practised by Sir Walter Raleigh, was better adapted, in its clinching final couplet, to the expression of moral truths.

Sir Walter Raleigh

FAREWELL TO THE COURT

THIS poem, in the spirit of Ovid's *Tristia*, was first published in *The Phoenix Nest* (1593). Raleigh was a proud man, but introspective about his misfortunes, brought about by disfavour with the Queen. To his melancholy he gives a romantic touch by identifying it with the changes of the seasons, his end being foreseen in the cold of winter.

Like truthles dreames, so are my joyes expired,
And past returne, are all my dandled daies:
My love misled, and fancie quite retired,
Of all which past, the sorow onely staies.

5 My lost delights now cleane from sight of land,
Have left me all alone in unknowne waies:
My minde to woe, my life in fortunes hand,
Of all which past, the sorow onely staies.

As in a countrey strange without companion,
10 I onely waile the wrong of deaths delaies,
Whose sweete spring spent, whose sommer well nie don,
Of all which past, the sorow onely staies.

Whom care forewarnes, ere age and winter colde,
To haste me hence, to find my fortunes folde.

2 *dandled:* spoilt, pampered, as when a child is humoured upon the knee.

4 *Of all which past, the sorow onely staies:* This refrain is the same as line 123 of the MS. of *Cynthia*, and is enlarged upon in Raleigh's *The History of the World*, I. 60.

10 *onely:* solitary, alone.

14 *my fortunes folde:* his country seat at Sherborne. In a letter to Lord Cecil of May 10, 1593, Raleigh uses this phrase, referring to his estate.

John Milton

WHEN THE ASSAULT WAS INTENDED TO YE CITTY

THIS sonnet (published 1645) was written in 1642, shortly after the battle of
Edgehill, when the Royalist army approached London; it was turned
back by Essex and his Roundheads. Milton anticipates the capture of London
and the entry of his home in Aldersgate Street. The octave is a plea for
mercy, usually granted in classical times to renowned poets. One manu-
script, not in Milton's hand, says that the sonnet was left on Milton's door
"when ye Citty expected an assault".

> Captain or Colonel, or Knight in Arms,
> Whose chance on these defenceless dores may sease,
> If deed of honour did thee ever please,
> Guard them, and him within protect from harms,
> 5   He can requite thee, for he knows the charms
> That call Fame on such gentle acts as these,
> And he can spred thy Name o're Lands and Seas,
> What ever clime the Suns bright circle warms.
> Lift not thy spear against the Muses Bowre,
> 10   The great Emathian Conqueror bid spare
> The house of Pindarus, when Temple and Towre
> Went to the ground: And the repeated air
> Of sad Electra's Poet had the power
> To save th' Athenian Walls from ruine bare.

1 *Colonel:* This was pronounced as a trisyllable in Milton's time.

5 *charms:* magic verses, from Latin *carmina*.

10 *The great Emathian Conqueror:* Alexander the Great, who came from
the Province of Emathia in Macedonia.

11 *The house of Pindarus:* Pindar's home was spared by Alexander when
he sacked Thebes in 333 B.C.

12 *repeated:* recited.

13 *sad Electra's Poet:* Euripides. The epithet "sad" refers to the play, not
the dramatist.

14 *To save th' Athenian Walls from ruine bare:* In 404 B.C. the Lacedae-
monians took Athens, and their Theban allies, out of jealousy, wanted the
city destroyed. According to Plutarch, in his life of the victorious general,
Lysander, the famous city was spared at a banquet, when the conquerors
heard the first chorus of *Electra* recited.

TO MY FRIEND MR. HENRY LAWES

THERE are three manuscripts of this poem, two in Milton's hand. The sonnet was written in 1646 and prefixed to the book *Choice Psalms put into Musick for three voices* (1648) by Henry and William Lawes. Lines 3, 6, 8, 12 and 13 were much improved by Milton, after his first draft; the original text is given on p. 322 of Helen Darbishire's edition. Henry Lawes (1595-1662) was Gentleman of the King's Chapel in the reign of Charles I, and a friend of Milton, in spite of his Royalist sympathies. In 1634 he had composed the music for the production of *Comus* at Ludlow Castle, himself presenting, acting in, and sponsoring the printing of the masque in 1637. His advance in composition was to suit the music to the meaning, vowel quantity and accentuation of the words. He composed for several poets, including Carew, Herrick and Waller.

    Harry whose tuneful and well measur'd Song
       First taught our English Musick how to span
       Words with just note and accent, not to scan
       With Midas Ears, committing short and long;
5   Thy worth and skill exempts thee from the throng,
       With praise anough for Envy to look wan;
       To after-age thou shalt be writ the man,
       That with smooth aire couldst humor best our tongue.
    Thou honour'st Verse, and Verse must lend her wing
10   To honour thee, the Priest of Phoebus Quire

2 *span:* measure, assess.

4 *With Midas Ears:* Ovid in *Metamorphoses,* XI. 146-79 tells how Apollo changed the ears of Midas into those of an ass, when he adjudged Pan to be his superior in song.   *committing:* making incongruous. Milton refers to the insensitive ears of those who do not perceive the poet's purpose in modulating the rhythm by opposing the metrical pattern.

5 *exempts thee from the song:* suggested by Horace *Odes,* I. 1. 32 (to Maecenas).

6 *anough:* This is Milton's usual spelling.

7 *thou shalt be writ:* suggested by Horace *Odes,* I. 6. 1 (to Agrippa).

10 *the Priest of Phoebus Quire:* The priest here is Lawes himself, and "Phoebus Quire" refers to the poets he composed for. The reference is to the sanctuary of Apollo at Delphi.

That tun'st their happiest lines in Hymn, or Story.
Dante shall give Fame leave to set thee higher
   Then his Casella, whom he woo'd to sing,
   Met in the milder shades of Purgatory.

11 *their:* the poets'.   *Story:* In 1653 Lawes set to music a narrative poem, Cartwright's *Complaint of Ariadne deserted by Theseus.*

12-13 *Dante . . . Casella:* Casella was a musician and friend of Dante, whom he met again among the souls in Purgatory (*Purgatorio*, II. 76-114), and persuaded to sing a canzone of the poet's composing.

14 *milder:* The precincts of Purgatory were more temperate than those of Inferno.

LAWRENCE OF VERTUOUS FATHER VERTUOUS SON

THIS sonnet, probably written in 1655, was first published in the 1673 (2nd) edition of Milton's *Poems*. The little-known Edward Lawrence was a friend of Milton during the Commonwealth, and the son of Henry, Lord President of the Council of Oliver Cromwell (1654-9). The poem is an epistle of invitation in the style of Horace. Milton apparently requests Lawrence to dine with him at home, as winter now prevents them from walking in the countryside together.

Lawrence of vertuous Father vertuous Son,
   Now that the Fields are dank, and ways are mire,
   Where shall we sometimes meet, and by the fire
   Help wast a sullen day; what may be won
5 From the hard Season gaining: time will run
   On smoother, till Favonius re-inspire
   The frozen earth; and cloath in fresh attire
   The Lillie and Rose, that neither sow'd nor spun.
   What neat repast shall feast us, light and choice,
10   Of Attick tast, with Wine, whence we may rise

1 Suggested by Horace *Odes*, I. 16. 1.

4 *wast:* spend.

6 *Favonius:* from Horace *Odes*, I. 4. 1: the gentle west wind of spring, also called Zephyrus.

9 *neat repast:* tasty meal.

10 *Attick:* refined, yet simple.

To hear the Lute well toucht, or artfull voice
Warble immortal Notes and Tuskan Ayre?
He who of those delights can judge, and spare
To interpose them oft, is not unwise.

13-14 *spare/To interpose:* refrain from indulging in.

MEDITATIONS

THE heading chosen for the third division of classical poetry in English is a convenient, though not an arbitrary one. It comprehends no recognizable *forms* of poetry, but illustrates rather the *voice* of the poet, assumed for different purposes and often addressed to different audiences.

In the style of the verse there is naturally overlapping with the first division of this collection, dominated by the epigram. What determines the class "meditations" is the discursive quality of the thinking. In differing humanistic spirit, it is found among the Greeks in Plato, Lucian and Plutarch; among the Romans in Lucretius, Vergil, Horace and Seneca; and in the Middle Ages in Boethius, Dante and Chaucer. Most of these writers exerted some influence on the choice of classical themes for poetry in the sixteenth and seventeenth centuries.

9. MONOLOGUES

THE clue is to be found in T. S. Eliot's essay "The Three Voices of Poetry": (1) "the voice of the poet talking to himself—or to nobody"; (2) "the voice of the poet addressing an audience, whether large or small". Eliot's third voice is, of course, the impersonal dialogue of dramatic representation.

Eliot says of the first voice that it is recognized by "the way it sounds when you read it [the poem] to yourself . . . what the reader will get from it is not paramount". Here he has in mind, I think, certain strains of the lyric voice of poets. The first sub-section (monologues) is, however, concerned with verse in which the poet himself, or an assumed personality, reflects aloud, not necessarily in rhythms that invite musical accompaniment. There is resemblance to the commentary of a Greek dramatic chorus, to the moral ode, and to the Elizabethan soliloquy. But, as Eliot says, "the 'psychic material' tends to create its own form".

The criterion here is that the poem is a *moral reflection overheard*, not actually intended by the poet for the ear of a single person. Even Campion's "A secret love" is a dramatic monologue of the type Ezra Pound calls a *persona* or mask, though not as arresting as Browning's. Here, says Eliot, the poet speaks in his second voice, "making imaginary persons talk poetry".

Thomas Wyatt

PATIENCE

THE form of this complaint is lyrical, the tone moral. The poet disciplines himself to rise above rejection by those who once esteemed him. This is a note more nobly struck by Wyatt than by the self-pitying Raleigh. The spirit of the poem is French and Italian; but the expression derives ultimately from Catullus, who was disappointed in the amoral Lesbia, Horace, who chose friendship and peace of mind rather than social position, Ovid of the *Tristia*, and Martial, the neglected poet of a materialistic age. Wyatt's stoic philosophy was strongly influenced by his reading of Boethius's *Consolations of Philosophy*.

> Patience, though I have not
>   The thing that I require,
> I must of force, god wot,
>   Forbere my moost desire;
> 5   For no ways can I fynde
>   To saile against the wynde.
>
> Patience, do what they will
>   To worke me woo or spite,
> I shall content me still
> 10   To thyncke boeth daye and nyte,
>   To thyncke and hold my peace,
>   Syns there is no redresse.
>
> Patience, withouten blame
>   For I offended nought;
> 15   I know they knowe the same,
>   Though they have chaunged their thought.
>   Was ever thought so moved
>   To hate that it haith loved?

4 *moost:* greatest.
7, 15, 16 *they:* his enemies who were once his friends.

Patience of all my harme,
20   For fortune is my foo;
Patience must be the charme
To hele me of my woo:
Patience withoute offence
Is a painfull patience.

20 *fortune is my foo:* "Fortune my foe" was a favourite tag among luck-less Elizabethans, and is probably of mediaeval origin.

Thomas Campion

A SECRET LOVE OR TWO I MUST CONFESSE

THE speaker is here a married light-of-love who justifies promiscuity by her readiness to meet her marital obligations. The monologue is ironically amusing in the logical analogies of its special pleading. But the verse is uncertain in its accentuation and rhythm, mainly where the rhyming lines have double endings. This may be due to Campion's alleged practice of setting words to music.

A secret love or two I must confesse
I kindly welcome for change in close playing,
Yet my deare husband I love ne'erthelesse,
His desires, whole or halfe, quickly allaying,
5   At all times ready to offer redresse:
His owne he never wants but hath it duely,
He twits me I keepe not touch with him truly.

The more a spring is drawne the more it flowes,
No Lampe less light retaines by lightning others:
10   Is hee a looser his losse that nere knowes?
Or is he wealthy that wast treasure smothers?
My churl vowes no man shall sent his sweet Rose,
His owne enough and more I give him duely,
Yet still he twits mee I keepe not touch truly.

2 *close playing:* There is a pun intended, since in music this referred to a method of fingering. But *close* also meant "secret", "available only to the privileged".

12 *churl:* Note the change of tone, after "deare husband" in the first stanza.

15 Wise Archers beare more than one shaft to field,
    The Venturer loads not with one ware his shipping;
Should Warriers learn but one weapon to weilde,
    Or thrive faire plants e'er the worse for the slipping?
One dish cloyes, many fresh appetite yeeld:
20   Mine own Ile use, and his he shall have duely,
    Judge then what debter can keep touch more truly.

16 *The Venturer:* usually a member of the Merchant Venturers, who took shared risks in sending ships abroad for merchandise. There may be a pun here, since *venturer* could also mean "strumpet".

18 *slipping:* taking slips or cuttings. A pun seems intended here.

Ben Jonson

TO THE WORLD. A FAREWELL FOR A GENTLE-WOMAN VERTUOUS AND NOBLE

In this dramatic monologue, the poet speaks bitterly of the world on behalf of a misanthropic lady, whose identity has not been traced. The poem is not only a stoical refusal to accept old age, but an exposure of the worldly life by one who has been through the mill. There is more of the cynicism of Diogenes than of the idealism of Cicero's *De Senectute*.

False world, good-night: since thou hast brought
    That houre upon my morne of age,
Hence-forth I quit thee from my thought,
    My part is ended on thy stage.
5   Doe not once hope, that thou canst tempt
    A spirit so resolv'd to tread
Upon thy throate, and live exempt
    From all the nets that thou canst spread.
I know thy formes are studyed arts,
10   Thy subtle wayes, be narrow straits;
Thy curtesie but sodaine starts,
    And what thou call'st thy gifts are baits.

2 *morne of age:* probably a reference to the climacteric or critical period of life.

        I know too, though thou strut, and paint,
            Yet art thou both shrunke up, and old,
15   That onely fooles make thee a saint,
            And all thy good is to be sold.
        I know thou whole art but a shop
            Of toyes, and trifles, traps, and snares,
        To take the weake, or make them stop:
20   Yet art thou falser then thy wares.
        And, knowing this, should I yet stay,
            Like such as blow away their lives,
        And never will redeeme a day,
            Enamor'd of their golden gyves?
25   Or, having scap'd, shall I returne,
            And thrust my necke into the noose,
        From whence, so lately, I did burne,
            With all my powers, my selfe to loose?
        What bird, or beast, is knowne so dull,
30   That fled his cage, or broke his chaine,
        And tasting ayre, and freedome, wull
            Render his head in there againe?
        If these, who have but sense, can shun
            The engines, that have them annoy'd;
35   Little, for me, had reason done,
            If I could not thy ginnes avoyd.
        Yes, threaten, doe. Alas I feare
            As little, as I hope from thee:
        I know thou canst nor shew, nor beare
40   More hatred, then thou hast to mee.
        My tender, first, and simple yeeres
            Thou did'st abuse, and then betray;
        Since stird'st up jealousies and feares,
            When all the causes were away.

---

24 *gyves:* fetters.   **27** *burne:* desire.

31 *wull:* a common pronunciation, but here a visual rhyme to match
"dull".

32 *Render:* put back.   **33** *sense:* "the power of sensation", not reason.

34 *engines:* traps.   **36** *ginnes:* snares.

45   Then, in a soile hast planted me,
        Where breathe the basest of thy fooles;
     Where envious arts professed be,
        And pride, and ignorance the schooles,
     Where nothing is examin'd, weigh'd,
50   But, as 'tis rumor'd, so beleev'd:
     Where every freedome is betray'd,
        And every goodnesse tax'd, or griev'd.
     But, what we'are borne for, we must beare:
        Our fraile condition it is such,
55   That, what to all may happen here,
        If't chance to me, I must not grutch.
     Else, I my state should much mistake,
        To harbour a divided thought
     From all my kinde: that, for my sake,
60   There should a miracle be wrought.
     No, I doe know, that I was borne
        To age, misfortune, sicknesse, griefe:
     But I will beare these, with that scorne,
        As shall not need thy false reliefe.
65   Nor for my peace will I goe farre,
        As wandrers doe, that still doe rome,
     But make my strengths, such as they are,
        Here in my bosome, and at home.

45 *soile:* environment (possibly that of the Court).
52 *griev'd:* made the cause of regret.
56 *grutch:* complain.

HIS EXCUSE FOR LOVING

THIS is the first of a group of ten poems in celebration of *Charis*, a lady who has not been identified. They were published by Sir Kenelm Digby, as part of a collection called *Underwood*, in the second folio of 1640-1, and are a counterpart to Act III, scene 2 of *The New Inne* (1629). The mood of this poem, which is an address to the reader (line 13), has been described as one of "playful urbanity". Jonson insists that the language of love-poetry should be truthful (line 10), and indirectly reflects upon the extravagances of Petrarchism and Neoplatonism. But he had obviously been reading the fourth book of Castiglione's *The Courtier*, in which the right of an old man to contend in the Court of Love is defended. Jonson half amusingly, half seriously, maintains the convention. Similarly, in Horace *Odes*, IV. 1, the poet asks Venus whether a man of fifty years should enter the lists of love. Horace pretends that he is past passion, and writes to celebrate love as an ideal power; but he does not conceal that his praise is no academic exercise.

> Let it not your wonder move,
> Lesse your laughter; that I love.
> Though I now write fiftie yeares,
> I have had, and have my Peeres;
> 5 Poëts, though divine, are men:
> Some have lov'd as old agen.
> And it is not alwayes face,
> Clothes, or Fortune gives the grace;
> Or the feature, or the youth:
> 10 But the Language, and the Truth,
> With the Ardor, and the Passion,
> Gives the Lover weight, and fashion.
> If you then will read the Storie,
> First, prepare you to be sorie,
> 15 That you never knew till now
> Either whom to love, or how:
> But be glad, as soone with me,
> When you know, that this is she,
> Of whose Beautie it was sung,
> 20 She shall make the old man young,
> Keepe the middle age at stay,
> And let nothing high decay,
> Till she be the reason why,
> All the world for love may die.

9 *feature:* good looks.

CHARIS, HER MAN DESCRIBED BY HER OWNE DICTAMEN

THIS is the ninth poem in the Charis series, and in it Jonson adopts the *persona* of the lady herself. This leads to some interesting self-criticism; for Jonson is not the type she desires, a courtier, but a mocker of courtly affectations. Charis is, nevertheless, a woman of sprightly charm and moderate tastes; but she does not disapprove worldly enhancements, such as dress and titles. Whatever he offers of more solid parts in "His Excuse for loving", she declines as trivial substitutes, when compared with youth. The qualities Charis extolls are all catalogued in Castiglione's *The Courtier.*

Of your Trouble, Ben, to ease me,
I will tell what Man would please me.
I would have him, if I could,
Noble; or of greater Blood;
5   Titles, I confesse, doe take me;
And a woman God did make me:
French to boote, at least in fashion,
And his Manners of that Nation.
    Young I'ld have him to(o), and faire,
10   Yet a man; with crisped haire
Cast in thousand snares, and rings
For Loves fingers, and his wings;
Chestnut colour, or more slack
Gold, upon a ground of black.
15   Venus, and Minerva's eyes,
For he must looke wanton-wise.
    Eye-brows bent like Cupids bow,
Front, an ample field of snow;
Even nose, and cheeke (withall)
20   Smooth as is the Billiard Ball:
Chin, as woolly as the Peach;
And his lip should kissing teach,
Till he cherish'd too much beard,
And make Love or me afeard.

Title *Dictamen:* pronouncement.

4 *greater Blood:* princely descent.

7 *French to boote:* He should also resemble the French.

10 *crisped:* curly.

12 *his wings:* The reference is to Cupid.

13 *more slack:* not so dark.

14 *Gold, upon a ground of black:* The description is heraldic, in keeping with the man's status. What is probably implied is dark hair with highlights in it.

15 *Venus, and Minerva's eyes:* In the tapestries, which provided most of the representations of these goddesses, the eyes were usually blue.

18 *Front:* forehead.

20 *the Billiard Ball:* The game of billiards seems to have been introduced from France about the middle of the sixteenth century. The first reference to it in the *O.E.D.* is in *Mother Hubberds Tale* of Spenser (1591).

25　He would have a hand as soft
　　As the Downe, and shew it oft;
　　Skin as smooth as any rush,
　　And so thin, to see a blush
　　Rising through it e're it came;
30　All his blood should be a flame
　　Quickly fir'd, as in beginners
　　In loves schoole, and yet no sinners.
　　　　'Twere to(o) long, to speake of all:
　　What we harmonie doe call
35　In a body, should be there.
　　Well he should his clothes to(o) weare;
　　Yet no Taylor help to make him;
　　Drest, you still for man should take him;
　　And not thinke h'had eat a stake,
40　Or were set up in a Brake.
　　　　Valiant he should be as fire,
　　Shewing danger more than ire.
　　Bounteous as the clouds to earth;
　　And as honest as his Birth.
45　All his actions to be such,
　　As to doe no thing too much.
　　Nor o're-praise, nor yet condemne;
　　Nor out-valew, nor contemne;
　　Nor doe wrongs, nor wrongs receave;
50　Nor tie knots, nor knots unweave;
　　And from basenesse to be free,
　　As he durst love Truth and me.
　　　　Such a man, with every part,
　　I could give my very heart;
55　But of one, if short he came,
　　I can rest me where I am.

39 *h'had eat a stake:* bore himself so stiffly.

40 *set up in a Brake:* held in a frame; cf. *Silent Woman,* IV. 6. 583.

42 *danger:* boldness.

55 *But of one, if short he came:* i.e. if he were wanting in any of these qualities.

Henry King

A CONTEMPLATION UPON FLOWERS

THIS poem is ascribed to King in the British Museum Harleian MS. 6917, which contains other verse of his, as well as some family records. But the "Contemplation" is still regarded as doubtful by the editor of the "Nonesuch" collection, John Sparrow (1925), not being found in the reliable Phillips, Malone and Hannah MSS. King is a difficult author to assess, because he is steeped in several Elizabethan traditions. He resembles Donne in his preference for colloquial rhythms, and his oblique, but arresting, use of metaphor. The language of this poem, however, has a classical simplicity; only the phrases "Embroiderd garments" and "perfume my death" suggest metaphysical influence.

<blockquote>

Brave flowers, that I could gallant it like you
And be as little vaine;
You come abroad, and make a harmelesse shew,
And to your bedds of Earth againe;
5 You are not proud, you know your birth
For your Embroiderd garments are from Earth:

You doe obey your moneths, and times, but I
Would have it ever springe,
My fate would know noe winter, never dye
10 Nor thinke of such a thing;
Oh that I could my bed of Earth but view
And Smile, and looke as chearefully as you:

Oh teach me to see death, and not to feare
But rather to take truce;
15 How often have I seene you at a Beere,
And there looke fresh and spruce;
You fragrant flowers then teach me that my breath
Like yours may sweeten, and perfume my death.

</blockquote>

6 *Embroiderd garments:* bright variegated colours, as in needlework.
7 *moneths:* pronounced as a monosyllable.
14 *take truce:* to see death as a respite from something irksome.

Andrew Marvell

THE GARDEN

DOUGLAS BUSH in his *English Literature in the Earlier Seventeenth Century* speaks of Marvell's "capacity for sensuous identification with natural things". He disliked both the artificial life of cities and courts, and the formal garden. The baroque planning of the landscape-garden was making its appearance in England from France and Italy. There is evidence from content and versification that Marvell had read Cowley's "The Wish" before writing "The Garden". The Garden is the symbol of the perfect state from which Man fell in his desire for knowledge. Marvell does not point a moral of intellectual seriousness, but of quietude. The poem has what Hazlitt called "witty delicacy"; and T. S. Eliot describes Marvell's wit as classic, "an equipoise, a balance and proportion of tones". He says this is neither erudition nor cynicism; "it belongs to an educated mind, rich in generations of experience". Stephen Spender in his essays *The Making of a Poem*, comparing the classic with the romantic aim, says: "The classic landscape is nature tamed to be garden. The Romantic is garden in which the flowers are forced to grow wild." In "The Garden" Marvell presented one of the finest creative examples of the Christian humanism of the Renaissance, which sought to reconcile the real with the divine, the temporal with the eternal, nature with a state of grace, and reason with faith. The same idea lies behind Milton's *Comus*. Milton and Marvell, both Puritans, were interesting phenomena, trying to combat the rational dualism of Bacon with the divine illumination of Plato.

> How vainly men themselves amaze
> To win the Palm, the Oke, or Bayes;
> And their uncessant Labours see
> Crown'd from some single Herb or Tree,
> 5   Whose short and narrow verged Shade
> Does prudently their Toyles upbraid;
> While all Flow'rs and all Trees do close
> To weave the Garlands of repose.

1 *themselves amaze:* drive themselves stupid.

2 *the Oke:* The garland of oak leaves was awarded to a hero who saved a citizen's life in battle.   *Bayes:* laurel wreath.

5 *narrow verged Shade:* This refers to the angle of declination of the sun, which controls the extent of the shadow.

7-8 All plants and trees in the garden unite to provide man with peace of mind.

Garder

uv.24.
30

      Fair quiet, have I found thee here,
10   And Innocence thy Sister dear!
      Mistaken long, I sought you then
      In busie Companies of Men.
      Your sacred Plants, if here below,
      Only among the Plants will grow.
15   Society is all but rude,
      To this delicious Solitude.

      No white nor red was ever seen
      So am'rous as this lovely green.
      Fond Lovers, cruel as their Flame,
20   Cut in these Trees their Mistress name.
      Little, Alas, they know, or heed,
      How far these Beauties Hers exceed!
      Fair Trees! where s'eer your barkes I wound,
      No Name shall but your own be found.

25   When we have run our Passions heat,
      Love hither makes his best retreat.
      The Gods, that mortal Beauty chase,
      Still in a Tree did end their race.
      Apollo hunted Daphne so,
30   Only that She might Laurel grow.
      And Pan did after Syrinx speed,
      Not as a Nymph, but for a Reed.

13 *sacred Plants:* This phrase looks back to the Garden of Eden, suggested by "Innocence" in line 10.

15 *Society is all but rude:* Marvell suggests that a love of solitude is the mark of a civilized mind, not the quest for society.

19 *Flame:* passion.

22-4 Marvell says that the beauties of nature surpass those of woman; and that therefore he will not carve any woman's name on a tree.

27-30 The story of Apollo and Daphne, who was turned into a laurel, is told in Ovid's *Metamorphoses*, I. 5. Daphne was the daughter of the river-god Peneus in Thessaly.

31-2 The escape of Syrinx from Pan, by begging the gods to change her to a river-reed, is narrated in the same book of the *Metamorphoses*. The Arcadian nymph was a daughter of the river-god Ladon.

What wond'rous Life in this I lead!
Ripe Apples drop about my head;
35   The Luscious Clusters of the Vine
Upon my Mouth do crush their Wine;
The Nectaren, and curious Peach,
Into my hands themselves do reach;
Stumbling on Melons, as I pass,
40   Insnar'd with Flow'rs, I fall on Grass.

Mean while the Mind, from pleasure less,
Withdraws into its happiness:
The Mind, that Ocean where each kind
Does streight its own resemblance find;
45   Yet it creates, transcending these,
Far other Worlds, and other Seas;
Annihilating all that's made
To a green Thought in a green Shade.

37 *curious Peach:* The word *curious* here has its original meaning of "that which requires care". All the fruits mentioned in this stanza need man's cultivation and protection to thrive in England; it is not this kind of care that Marvell objects to.

38 Marvell believes that Nature provides for man without his effort, if he can only live in a state of innocence. This is the substance of the next stanza. "The Garden" was written before *Paradise Lost*.

41 *from pleasure less:* from a smaller pleasure (i.e. to a greater—its own happiness).

43-4 A reference to Sir Thomas Browne's *Pseudodoxia Epidemica* (1646). "That all Animals of the Land, are in their kinde in the sea" is one of the vulgar errors which the antiquary refutes. Hence the reference to the mind as an ocean.

47-8 The meaning of these lines is discussed in William Empson's *Some Versions of Pastoral*. A "green Thought" seems to be a "virile idea", something with creative potentiality; "green Shade" (Vergil's *viridi umbra*) is obvious. In the anonymous play *Edward III* there are found the lines:

Since green our thoughts, green be the conventicle
Where we will ease us by disburdening 'em.

Marvell says that the mind of man is capable of anything, and can "annihilate" (or deny) limitations of the material world.

Here at the Fountains sliding foot,
50 Or at some Fruit-trees mossy root,
Casting the Bodies Vest aside,
My Soul into the boughs does glide:
There like a Bird it sits, and sings,
Then whets, and combs its silver Wings;
55 And, till prepar'd for longer flight,
Waves in its Plumes the various Light.

Such was that happy Garden-state,
While Man there walk'd without a Mate:
After a Place so pure, and sweet,
60 What other Help could yet be meet!
But 'twas beyond a Mortal's share
To wander solitary there:
Two Paradises 'twere in one
To live in Paradise alone.

65 How well the skilful Gardner drew
Of flow'rs and herbes this Dial new;

51 *the Bodies Vest:* the physical self.

52-4 This beautiful conceit has something of Platonic mysticism in it; but this is curbed by Marvell's Puritan faith in the literal truth of the Bible, which is shown in the next stanza, in which the loss of man's bliss is explained by the advent of woman in the garden.

54 *whets:* preens.

55 *till prepar'd for longer flight:* referring to the soul's destination in Heaven.

60 *What other Help could yet be meet:* The word *meet* means "fitting", but the poet here puns on the word *helpmeet*, the original form of *helpmate*.

61 *share:* capacity.

63-4 The intellectual concept here is metaphysical. It is advanced in the final stanza of the poem.

65 *the skilful Gardner:* an oblique reference to God. In this world the skill is shown by the horiculturist who can plan a garden in which flowers will open and close in rotation, at the appropriate time of the day. The art is referred to in Mrs. Heman's *Dial of Flowers* and Charlotte Smith's *Horologe of the Field*; Linnaeus had such a flower-dial of forty-six varieties. The idea is expanded in Marvell's Latin version of the poem, called *Hortus*.

66 *this Dial new:* The poet supposes the possibility of a second Paradise for man in the garden.

Where from above the milder Sun
Does through a fragrant Zodiack run;
And, as it works, th' industrious Bee
70   Computes its time as well as we.
How could such sweet and wholsome Hours
Be reckon'd but with herbs and flow'rs!

68 *a fragrant Zodiack:* "fragrant" because of the flowers of which the Dia l
is composed. The Zodiack was the name given in ancient times to the
twelve constellations, each occupying about 30 degrees, through which the
Sun's course passed during the seasons of the year.

Abraham Cowley

OF MYSELF

As early as the publication of *The Mistress* (1647), Cowley had longed for a
peaceful country retreat with the joys of a garden. 'The Wish' was a poem
in which he expressed the rural sentiment admirably. In his biography of
Abraham Cowley, Thomas Sprat tempers the final eulogy with regret that
the poet should end his days in the deliberate obscurity of retirement. Sprat
writes: "It is certainly a great disparagement to Vertue and Learning it self,
that those very things which only make men useful in the World, should
encline them to leave it." Cowley's *Essays* are mainly the fruit of this period
at Chertsey. An autobiographical one includes this poem, being the final
three stanzas of an ode which the poet says he wrote at thirteen. The
conclusion, he admits, is taken from Horace, *Odes*, III. 29. 41-5, in which the
poet, writing to Maecenas, accepts the precept *carpe diem* of Epicurus.
Horace writes: "Calmly to deal with the present is wisdom; for life is like a
river and moves along uncontrolled." After Horace, Cowley loved Spenser,
whose *Faerie Queene*, he says in the same essay, he had read at the age of
twelve. He concludes the discourse with a free translation of Martial,
Epigrams xlvii, Book 10, one of the most translated poems from Latin of
the sixteenth and seventeenth centuries.

This only grant me, that my Means may lye
Too low for Envy, for Contempt too high.
    Some Honor I would have
Not from Great deeds, but Good alone.
5   Th' unknown are better than ill known.
    Rumour can ope' the Grave,
Acquaintance I would have, but when 't depends
Not on the Number, but the Choice, of Friends.

Books should, not Business, entertain the Light,
10   And sleep, as undisturb'd as Death, the Night.
        My House a Cottage, more
Then Palace, and should fitting be
For all my Use, no Luxurie.
        My Garden painted o're
15   With Nature's hand, not Arts; and Pleasures yield,
Horace might envy in his Sabine field.

Thus would I double my Life's fading space,
For he that runs it well, twice runs his race.
        And in this true delight,
20   These unbought Sports, this happy State,
I would not fear nor wish my Fate,
        But boldly say each night,
To morrow let my Sun his Beams display,
Or in Clouds hide them; I have liv'd to Day.

10. DISCOURSES

MONTAIGNE and Bacon in the essay or "dispersed meditation", Sidney in
An Apology for Poetry, Castiglione in *The Courtier* (Englished by Sir Thomas
Hoby), all exemplified the public utterance or "goodly discourse" for the
cultured world. The counterparts in English classical verse were poems of a
discursive type, moral in their implications and distinguished in expression,
in the spirit of Horace's *Sermones*; or, if more exasperated, of Juvenal,
Martial, Petronius and the dialogues of Lucian. In near perfection, the type
is represented by Waller's "Of English Verse", Cleveland's "Antiplatonick",
Pope's *Essay on Criticism* and *Epistle to Dr. Arbuthnot*, and Johnson's *The
Vanity of Human Wishes*.

John Cleveland

THE ANTIPLATONICK

SAINTSBURY reprinted the 1653 version of this poem, which was slightly
revised in the edition of 1677. In his mood of half-seriousness, Cleveland is a
Cavalier poet, leaning, as George Williamson said, "in content toward
Donne, and in form toward Jonson". Dryden complained of Cleveland that

he "gives us many times a hard nut to break our teeth, without a kernel for our pains"; and he drew attention to his "common thoughts in abstruse words". Yet the images are often as piquant as fantastic. He is the arch-debunker among Restoration lyrists; for his levity suited the temper of the age. Irreverent treatment of the platonic in love, as in the first four lines, is not uncommon in Lucretius, Catullus and Martial. The first stanza sets the witty tone of the indifferent sensual man who was fashionable at the Courts of the Stuart kings.

> For shame, thou everlasting wooer,
> Still saying grace and never falling to her!
> Love that's in contemplation placed
> Is Venus drawn but to the waist.
> 5 Unless your flame confess its gender,
> And your parley cause surrender,
> Y'are salamanders of a cold desire
> That live untouched amidst the hottest fire.
>
> What though she be a dame of stone,
> 10 The widow of Pygmalion,
> As hard and unrelenting she
> As the new-crusted Niobe,
> Or (what doth more of statue carry)
> A nun of the Platonic quarry?

7-8 *salamanders of a cold desire:* In ancient belief the salamander, a lizard-like creature, could endure fire. But by 1700 the word had come by analogy to mean a woman able to live chastely among temptations. Cleveland here uses this symbol of heraldry for the male.

10 *The widow of Pygmalion:* Pygmalion was a royal sculptor of Cyprus who fell in love with an ivory (or marble) carving of his own making. He begged Aphrodite to breathe life into her, and then married her. The story is told in Ovid *Metamorphoses*, X; but there is no mention of the lady's widowhood. This is a touch added by Cleveland, who suggests that Pygmalion's love reverted to stone when he no longer embraced her.

12 *the new-crusted Niobe:* Niobe, daughter of King Tantalus of Lydia, married Amphion, by whom she had many sons and daughters. Her pride in her progeny invoked the anger of Latona, whose children, Apollo and Diana, killed all Niobe's offspring, save one daughter. The shock of this disaster turned Niobe to stone. "New-crusted" refers to the harshness of her exterior.

15 Love melts the rigour which the rocks have bred—
    A flint will break upon a feather-bed.

    For shame, you pretty female elves,
    Cease for to candy up your selves;
    No more, you sectaries of the game,
20 No more of your calcining flame!
    Women commence by Cupid's dart
    As a king hunting dubs a hart.
    Love's votaries enthral each other's soul,
    Till both of them live but upon parole.

25 Virtue's no more in womankind
    But the green-sickness of the mind;
    Philosophy (their new delight)
    A kind of charcoal appetite.
    There's no sophistry prevails
30 Where all-convincing love assails,
    But the disputing petticoat will warp,
    As skilful gamesters are to seek at sharp.

16 The wit of paradox is a favourite device of Cleveland and poets such as Suckling.

18 *candy up:* beautify.   **19** *sectaries:* heretics.

20 *calcining flame:* According to Holland's Pliny II. 599 the burning of stone to a fine powder to produce mortar was *calcining* it. The alchemists believed that minerals and metals were purified of baser matter by the treatment of flame. Calcination was the first of their five chemical operations, later extended by Geber to eight, and by Pernety to twelve.

22 *dubs:* strikes or stabs. But there is a pun here, as a king *dubs* (i.e. "confers an honour on") a knight. Women are ennobled by love, as the hart is honoured by a royal hunt.

23 *enthral:* enslave.

24 *parole:* promise or engagement given upon word of honour.

26 *green-sickness:* anaemia affecting girls at the age of puberty and giving them a slightly green colouring.

28 *A kind of charcoal appetite:* Charcoal (one of the supposed remedies for green-sickness) results from the imperfect combustion of wood. The suggestion is that philosophy is an imperfect substitute for love.

31 *the disputing petticoat will warp:* the learned woman will yield.

32 *As skilful gamesters are to seek at sharp:* The meaning given by Saintsbury is: As skilful fencers are not good at sword-play.

The soldier, that man of iron,
Whom ribs of horror all environ,
35   That's strung with wire instead of veins,
In whose embraces you're in chains,
Let a magnetic girl appear,
Straight he turns Cupid's cuirassier.
Love storms his lips, and takes the fortress in,
40   For all the bristled turnpikes of his chin.

Since love's artillery then checks
The breastworks of the firmest sex,
Come, let us in affections riot;
Th'are sickly pleasures keep a diet
45   Give me a lover bold and free,
Not eunuched with formality,
Like an ambassador that beds a queen
With the nice caution of a sword between.

33 *soldier:* The word is here trisyllabic.
38 *cuirassier:* cavalry soldier equipped with a metal corslet.
40 *turnpikes:* spiked barriers placed across roads.

Henry King

PARADOX. THAT FRUITION DESTROYS LOVE

THIS poem is an example of extended analogy in argument; but it shows an attenuated use of the conceits of Donne, because the intellect is seldom "at the tips of the senses". King has become a sententious moralist. The argument offered is the opposite of that used by Cleveland in the previous poem. King's management of the couplet for the purpose of dialectic is, nonetheless, skilful.

Love is our Reasons Paradox, which still
Against the judgment doth maintain the Will:
And governs by such arbitrary laws,
It onely makes the Act our Likings cause:

1 *our Reasons Paradox:* "Paradox" means "contrary", because setting desire against reason.
2 *Will:* desire to possess.

5 We have no brave revenge, but to forgo
Our full desires, and starve the Tyrant so.

They whom the rising blood tempts not to taste,
Preserve a stock of Love can never waste;
When easie people who their wish enjoy,
10 Like Prodigalls at once their wealth destroy.
Adam till now had stayd in Paradise
Had his desires been bounded by his eyes.
When he did more then look, that made th' offence,
And forfeited his state of innocence.
15 Fruition therefore is the bane t'undoe
Both our affection and the subject too.
'Tis Love into worse language to translate,
And make it into Lust degenerate:
'Tis to De-throne, and thrust it from the heart,
20 To seat it grossely in the sensual part.
Seek for the Starre that's shot upon the ground,
And nought but a dimme gelly there is found.
Thus foul and dark our female starres appear,
If fall'n or loosned once from Vertues Sphear.
25 Glow-worms shine onely look't on, and let ly,
But handled crawl into deformity:
So beauty is no longer fair and bright,
Then whil'st unstained by the appetite:
And then it withers like a blasted flowre
30 Some poys'nous worm or spider hath crept ore.
Pigmaleon's dotage on the carved stone,
Shews Amorists their strong illusion.
Whil'st he to gaze and court it was content,
He serv'd as Priest at beauties Monument:
35 But when by looser fires t'embraces led,
It prov'd a cold hard Statue in his bed.

21-2 This is one of the vulgar errors, common in the poetry of the seventeenth century, that Sir Thomas Browne does not deal with.

31-6 No version of the Pygmalion story affirms the judgment made by King in these lines. Cf. Cleveland, "The Antiplatonick", line 10, *note*.

Irregular affects, like mad mens dreams
Presented by false lights and broken beams,
So long content us, as no neer address
40   Shews the weak sense our painted happiness.
But when those pleasing shaddowes us forsake,
Or of the substance we a trial make,
Like him, deluded by the fancies mock,
We ship-wrack 'gainst an Alabaster rock.
45   What though thy Mistress far from Marble be?
Her softness will transform and harden thee.
Lust is a Snake, and Guilt the Gorgons head,
Which Conscience turns to Stone and Joyes to Lead.

Turtles themselves will blush, if put to name
50   The Act, whereby they quench their am'rous flame.
Who then that's wise or vertuous, would not feare
To catch at pleasures which forbidden were,
When those which we count lawful, cannot be
Requir'd without some loss of modestie?
55   Ev'n in the Marriage-Bed, where soft delights
Are authoriz'd and customary Rites;
What are those tributes to the wanton sense,
But toleration of Incontinence?
For properly you cannot call that Love
60   Which does not from the Soul, but Humour move.

37 *affects:* phenomena.
39 *as no neer address:* that no closer inspection.
40 *painted:* illusory.
41 *shaddowes:* unrealities.
44 *'gainst an Alabaster rock:* against the cruel reality of the stone statue.
47 *the Gorgons head:* Ovid, *Metamorphoses*, IV. 5. 618. The Gorgons were three monstrous sisters, whose look turned beholders to stone. One of them, Medusa, was mortal, and because of a relationship with Neptune, Minerva turned her hair to writhing serpents. Perseus attacked the Gorgons and presented Medusa's head to the goddess.
49-50 *Turtles:* i.e. doves. The talking and blushing doves are a vulgar error used as a conceit.
60 *Humour:* disposition.

Thus they who worhip't Pan or Isis Shrine,
By the fair Front judg'd all within Divine:
Though entring, found 'twas but a Goat or Cow
To which before their ignorance did bow.
65 Such Temples and such Goddesses are these
Which foolish Lovers and admirers please:
Who if they chance within the Shrine to prie,
Find that a beast they thought a Deity.
Nor makes it onely our opinion less
70 Of what we lik't before, and now possess;
But robbs the Fuel, and corrupts the Spice
Which sweetens and inflames Loves sacrifice.
After Fruition once, what is Desire
But ashes kept warm by a dying fire?
75 This is (if any) the Philosophers Stone,
Which still miscarries at Projection.
For when the Heat ad Octo intermits,
It poorly takes us like Third Ague fits;

61 *Pan or Isis Shrine:* Both gods were of Egyptian origin, symbolized by the goat (or god of fecundity) and the cow (or god of fertility). Pan, the presiding deity of shepherds in Arcadia, was later adopted by the Romans, who honoured him at their Lupercalia.

71-2 *the Spice/Which sweetens:* The word spice originally covered sweet-meats and dried fruit (such as raisins). Sugar is Arabian in origin, and though not aromatic, was often used, like spice, as a preservative.

75 *the Philosophers Stone:* a solid substance which the alchemists thought possessed the property of turning other metals into gold or silver. Like the elixir, it could prolong life and cure diseases.

76 *Which still miscarries at Projection:* From the Philosopher's Stone the alchemists were to prepare a *Powder of Projection*, which would transmute baser metals into gold. But all experiments failed.

77 *the Heat ad Octo:* Alchemy, as explained by Geber, had ascending degrees of fire or heating, and used a variety of apparatus for the purpose. The science was still in use at the restoration of the English monarchy, but was given its death-blow by the publication of Robert Boyle's *The Sceptical Chymist* in 1661.

78 *Third Ague fits:* The "ague" or malarial fever was the first or hot paroxysm of the illness, the other two being the cold and sweating stages.

Or must on Embers as dull Druggs infuse,
80 Which we for Med'cine, not for Pleasure, use.

Since Lovers joyes then leave so sick a taste,
And soon as relish'd by the Sense are past;
They are but Riddles sure, lost if possest,
And therefore onely in Reversion best.
85 For bate them Expectation and Delay,
You take the most delightful Scenes away.
These two such rule within the fancie keep,
As banquets apprehended in our sleep;
After which pleasing trance next morn we wake
90 Empty and angry at the nights mistake.
Give me long Dreams and Visions of content,
Rather then pleasures in a minute spent.
And since I know before, the shedding Rose
In that same instant doth her sweetness lose,
95 Upon the Virgin-stock still let her dwell
For me, to feast my longings with her smell.
Those are but counterfeits of joy at best,
Which languish soon as brought unto the test.
Nor can I hold it worth his pains who tries
100 To Inne that Harvest which by reaping dies.

79 *Or must on Embers as dull Druggs infuse:* One of the objects of alchemy, as Paracelsus showed, was to produce medical drugs, the constituents being purified by calcination, sublimation, distillation, etc., using different processes of heat. The powdered ash after calcination of minerals was often "infused" into liquids, such as spirits of wine. "Alcohol" (al-kohl) was originally a cosmetic, the Arabic word for a metallic powder used by women to stain their eyelids.

83 *Riddles:* dark sayings, intentionally worded in a puzzling way, so as to compel guesswork. The meaning of "lost if possest" seems to be that the answer, if obtained, is quickly forgotten.

84 *And therefore onely in Reversion best:* In law, the phrase "in reversion" means the right to succeed to a place or emolument on the death or retirement of the holder. The meaning here seems to be that the pleasure of physical love is not in the act itself but in retrospect, and the anticipation of renewing it.

100 *To Inne:* to gather in.

Resolve me now what spirit hath delight,
If by full feed you kill the appetite?
That stomack healthy'st is, that nere was cloy'd,
Why not that Love the best then, nere enjoy'd?
105 Since nat'rally the blood, when tam'd or sated,
Will cool so fast it leaves the object hated.
Pleasures like wonders quickly lose their price
When Reason or Experience makes us wise.

To close my argument then. I dare say
110 (And without Paradox) as well we may
Enjoy our Love and yet preserve Desire,
As warm our hands by putting out the fire.

Edmund Waller

OF LOVE

THIS poem, in Waller's favourite metre, the octosyllabic couplet, typifies his method in the poetic discourse. The argument is in three parts: the first describing the uniqueness and servility of love among the emotions, ending in the analogy between successful courtship and the taming of a high-mettled horse. This idea of "government" leads on to the second part, a long comparison of the situations of women in the societies of East and West, suggesting with extended hyperbole that the sought-after aristocratic ladies of England were as tyrannical towards their suitors as the Turk in his despotic government. Waller ends with a sustained simile on the ironically despised male, in which he is now a stag run to earth by hunting dogs, scarcely with time enough to admire himself in the mirror. "Man the pursued" is a popular theme of the Cavalier love poet; it is also the germ of high-comedy in Congreve's *The Way of the World*.

Anger, in hasty words, or blows,
Itself discharges on our foes;
And sorrow too finds some relief
In tears, which wait upon our grief:
5 So every passion, but fond Love,
Unto its own redress does move:
But that alone the wretch inclines
To what prevents his own designs;

8 *prevents*: inhibits.

F

Makes him lament, and sigh, and weep
10   Disorder'd, tremble, fawn, and creep;
Postures which render him despis'd,
Where he endeavours to be priz'd.
For women (born to be control'd)
Stoop to the forward and the bold:
15   Affect the haughty and the proud,
The gay, the frolic, and the loud.
Who first the generous steed opprest,
Not kneeling did salute the beast;
But with high courage, life, and force,
20   Approaching, tam'd th' unruly horse.
Unwisely we the wiser East
Pity, supposing them opprest
With tyrants' force, whose law is will,
By which they govern, spoil, and kill:
25   Each nymph, but moderately fair,
Commands with no less rigor here.
Should some brave Turk, that walks among
His twenty lasses, bright and young;
And beckons to the willing dame,
30   Preferr'd to quench his present flame;
Behold as many Gallants here,
With modest guise, and silent fear,
All to one female idol bend:
While her high pride does scarce descend
35   To mark their follies; he would swear
That these her guard of eunuchs were:
And that a more majestic Queen,
Or humbler slaves, he had not seen.
All this with indignation spoke,
40   In vain I struggled with the yoke
Of mighty Love: that conquering look,

15 *Affect:* care for.
17 *generous steed:* Used in relation to domestic animals, *generous* meant "of good breed" in the seventeenth and eighteenth centuries. Cf. Pope. *Essay on Criticism,* 86–7.   *opprest:* trained, broke in.
23 *will:* lust.

When next beheld, like lightning strook
My blasted soul: and made me bow,
Lower than those I pity'd now.
45   So the tall stag, upon the brink
Of some smooth stream, about to drink,
Surveying there his armed head,
With shame remembers that he fled
The scorned dogs; resolves to try
50   The combat next: but, if their cry
Invades again his trembling ear,
He strait resumes his wonted care;
Leaves the untasted spring behind,
And, wing'd with fear, out-flies the wind.

42 *strook:* the commonest seventeenth-century spelling of the preterite *struck*, especially in verse.

47 *Surveying:* seeing reflected.

OF ENGLISH VERSE

THIS poem is an interesting commentary on the suitability of English as a poetic language in the seventeenth century. In the second and third stanzas Waller advances the well-thumbed argument of the classicists that the transitional and unformed nature of the language ("We write in sand") makes it unfit for literary permanence. Hence the tide of progress will obliterate such value as good writing may have, and its poetry can only be ephemeral. He speaks of Greek and Latin as having the fixity and durability of marble. In the fourth stanza Waller says that Chaucer survives only through the sense of his language, the art being lost in ignorance of the principles of his versification—a view that was echoed by Dryden. In the last two stanzas, the theory advanced is that Beauty aids the poet who is responsive to his age; even a meagre talent may preserve from complete oblivion a few transitory things, that are loved for their own sake.

Poets may boast, as safely vain,
Their works shall with the world remain:
Both bound together, live or die,
The verses and the prophecy.

4 *The verses and the prophecy:* The poet as prophet, much older than the hero-worship of Carlyle, is found not only in Milton and Shelley, but in ancient Greece, where the prophecies of oracles were delivered in hexameters.

5   But who can hope his line should long
     Last, in a daily-changing tongue?
     While they are new, envy prevails;
     And as that dies, our language fails.

     When architects have done their part,
10   The matter may betray their art:
     Time, if we use ill-chosen stone,
     Soon brings a well-built palace down.

     Poets that lasting marble seek,
     Must carve in Latin or in Greek;
15   We write in sand; our language grows,
     And, like the tide, our work o'erflows.

     Chaucer his sense can only boast;
     The glory of his numbers lost!
     Years have defac'd his matchless strain;
20   And yet he did not sing in vain.

     The beauties which adorn'd that age,
     The shining subjects of his rage,
     Hoping they should immortal prove,
     Rewarded with success his love.

25   This was the generous poet's scope;
     And all an English pen can hope;
     To make the Fair approve his flame,
     That can so far extend their fame.

6 *a daily-changing tongue:* The uncertainty of English grammar, spelling
and pronunciation was a frequent argument of detractors, when English
was defended as a literary language.

7-8 *While they are new, envy prevails:* Waller maintains that the interest
of English poetry is in its novelty and the rivalry of other poets. When
these pass, the work is forgotten.

22 *rage:* poetic emotions. Waller asserts that the art of Chaucer's age
crowned his achievements, because he was responsive to its spirit.

25 *generous:* noble.   27 *the Fair:* the fair *sex*.

Verse, thus design'd, has no ill fate,
30 If it arrive but at the date
Of fading beauty; if it prove
But as long-liv'd as present love.

UPON THE EARL OF ROSCOMMON'S TRANSLATION OF HORACE, *DE ARTE POETICA*: AND OF THE USE OF POETRY

WENTWORTH DILLON, Earl of Roscommon (1633-85), published his translation of the *Ars Poetica* in 1680, Waller's poem accompanying it. Roscommon also wrote "An Essay upon Translated Verse" and admired Milton's *Paradise Lost*. An interesting development in Waller's poem is the verse paragraphing, which Milton had employed in his epic. Waller enunciates the Augustan principles of correctness, of judgment restraining fancy, taken over from Boileau. He also notes the different functions of verse and prose, seeing the latter through the eyes of a member of the Royal Society. In the "true filed line" (Waller reminds us) Horace proved the guide of succeeding ages; he was a national poet who bestowed tributes where they were deserved (lines 29-36). The last paragraph recalls the humanizing effects of poetry illustrated in Greek mythology (lines 43-50). Waller echoes a passage near the end of Horace's epistle, in which the poet tells how Orpheus tamed wild beasts, and Amphion built the city of Thebes to the strain of his lyre. The final allusion to the bees is mainly from Vergil's *Georgics*, Book IV.

Rome was not better by her Horace taught,
Than we are here to comprehend his thought:
The Poet writ to noble Piso there;
A noble Piso does instruct us here:
5 Gives us a pattern in his flowing stile;
And with rich precepts does oblige our isle:
Britain! whose genius is in verse express'd;
Bold and sublime, but negligently dress'd.

3 *noble Piso:* The *Ars Poetica* was not a title that Horace gave to his verse treatise; it was written as an epistle of advice to the Pisos (father and two sons), who were noble because descended from Numa Pompilius.

8 *negligently dress'd:* This was the view generally taken by the Augustans of Elizabethan poetry—it "wanted art".

    Horace will our superfluous branches prune,
10 Give us new rules, and set our harp in tune;
    Direct us how to back the winged horse,
    Favour his flight, and moderate his force.
    Though Poets may of inspiration boast,
    Their rage, ill govern'd, in the clouds is lost.
15 He that proportion'd wonders can disclose,
    At once his fancy and his judgment shows.
    Chaste moral writing we may learn from hence;
    Neglect of which no wit can recompence.
    The fountain which from Helicon proceeds,
20 That sacred stream! should never water weeds;
    Nor make the crop of thorns and thistles grow,
    Which envy or perverted nature sow.
    Well-sounding verses are the charm we use,
    Heroic thoughts and virtue to infuse:
25 Things of deep sense we may in prose unfold;
    But they move more in lofty numbers told:
    By the loud trumpet, which our courage aids,
    We learn that sound, as well as sense, persuades.
    The Muse's friend, unto himself severe,
30 With silent pity looks on all that err:
    But where a brave, a public action shines,
    That he rewards with his immortal lines.
    Whether it be in council or in fight,
    His country's honour is his chief delight:
35 Praise of great acts he scatters as a seed,
    Which may the like in coming ages breed.
    Here taught the fate of verses (always priz'd

10 *Give us new rules:* Waller is here anticipating Pope's *Essay on Criticism*.

11 *to back the winged horse:* "back" means "mount and control". The "winged horse" is Pegasus, the striking of whose hoof upon the rock of Helicon caused the flowing of Hippocrene, fountain of the Muses. Pegasus is here the symbol of unrestrained inspiration.

17 *Chaste moral writing:* This was regarded by the Augustans as the supreme quality of Horace.

26 *But they move more in lofty numbers told:* suggesting that thoughts expressed in the rhythm of verse move more gracefully than in prose.

> With admiration, or as much despis'd)
> Men will be less indulgent to their faults;
> 40   And patience have to cultivate their thoughts.
> Poets lose half the praise they should have got,
> Could it be known what they discreetly blot:
> Finding new words, that to the ravish'd ear
> May like the language of the Gods appear:
> 45   Such, as of old, wise bards employ'd, to make
> Unpolish'd men their wild retreats forsake:
> Law-giving Heroes, fam'd for taming brutes,
> And raising cities with their charming lutes.
> For rudest minds with harmony were caught,
> 50   And civil life was by the Muses taught.
> So, wandering bees would perish in the air,
> Did not a sound, proportion'd to their ear,
> Appease their rage, invite them to the hive,
> Unite their force, and teach them how to thrive:
> 55   To rob the flowers, and to forbear the spoil;
> Preserv'd in winter by their summer's toil:
> They give us food, which may with nectar vie,
> And wax, that does the absent sun supply.

51-3 Plato in the *Ion* compares the souls of poets to bees; and Varro called bees the birds of the Muses. In the fourth Pythian Ode, Pindar speaks of the prophetess at Delphi as the "Delphic Bee". It was a common belief among the ancients that bees enjoyed the sense of hearing. Vergil refers to the clanging of cymbals to attract them to a hive when swarming, and it was a practice in the Roman Empire to beat a key on a warming-pan for the same purpose.

58 *And wax, that does the absent sun supply:* the wax being used for candles.

II. MORAL POEMS

F. R. LEAVIS, in his essay "Johnson and Augustanism" in *The Common Pursuit*, speaks of Johnson's "bondage . . . to moralistic fallacy and confusion" in not understanding "that works of art *enact* their moral valuations". The criticism overlooks the human situation, with its complex of disciplines, which for some students have values more compelling than the aesthetic. For the classical poets, poetry was intended to edify, to console the reader as well as to strengthen his moral attitudes. There have always been poets of this type, some more direct than others in the communication of their truths.

The modern critical taste is for an oblique or implied expression of morality, rather than didactic discourses. One or two of the poems here included are expressions of a personal philosophy, arising out of a disturbing accident of experience. Others speak of a settled way of life, in the spirit of Horace's discriminating asceticism, which leans more to the "golden mean" than to the abandonment of the world. The remainder speak of the security of faith and the religious attitude of mind. The poets write of "primitive and essential things" that, in the words of Max Beerbohm, "have great power to touch the heart of the beholder".

Sir Walter Raleigh

THE ADVICE

THE authority for this poem, and its title, is a volume which appeared in 1660, entitled *Le Prince d'Amour, or the Prince of Love, with a Collection of Several Ingenious Poems and Songs by the Wits of the Age*. The dedication makes clear that the expression "Wits of the Age" does not confine the poems to the reigns of the first two Stuart kings. The collection was made by a member of the Middle Temple, one of the Inns of Court that held their revels at Christmas. In the revels of 1598, Raleigh himself took part, according to Hoskins's *Directions for Speech and Style*. The initials W.R. are subscribed to the poem in MS. Rawlinson Poet. 85, as well as in the printed version of 1660. In the British Museum MS. addit. 22601, the poem is addressed to Mrs. Anne Vavasor, Maid of Honour to Queen Elizabeth and a celebrated beauty; though William Oldys, on the evidence of the printed poem only, believed it was addressed to Raleigh's wife. Miss Agnes Latham, in her edition of Raleigh's *Poems* for the "Muses Library" (1951), says that "the imagery of flowers, leaves and corn is characteristic of Raleigh", because it occurs also in 'Cynthia.' The song-like repetitions and refrains in lines 1, 3, 5 and 6 of each stanza are typical of Raleigh too, and of the French courtly tradition.

> Many desire, but few or none deserve
> To win the Fort of thy most constant will:
> Therefore take heed, let fancy never swerve
> But unto him that will defend thee still.
> 5   For this be sure, the fort of fame once won,
> Farewell the rest, thy happy dayes are done.

5 *fame:* reputation.

Many desire, but few or none deserve
To pluck the flowers and let the leaves to fall;
Therefore take heed, let fancy never swerve,
10   But unto him that will take leaves and all.
     For this be sure, the flower once pluckt away,
     Farewell the rest, thy happy days decay.

Many desire, but few or none deserve
To cut the corn, not subject to the sickle.
15   Therefore take heed, let fancy never swerve,
     But constant stand for Mowers mindes are fickle.
     For this be sure, the crop being once obtain'd
     Farewell the rest, the soil will be disdain'd.

16 The Mower image anticipates those of the interesting group of Mower poems by Marvell.

Robert Southwell, S.J.

SOUTHWELL, who joined the Jesuit order at the age of seventeen, came of an old aristocratic family that had connections with the Cecils, the Bacons and with the ancestors of Percy Bysshe Shelley. He was born at Horsham St. Faith near Norwich, and educated abroad by the Jesuits of Douai, Paris and Rome, his facility in Latin being equal to that in English. In spite of his European training, he preferred traditional English measures to French and Italian ones, and had the honour of being the first religious mystic in the simple vernacular, without the technical versatility of his successors, Herbert, Vaughan, Crashaw and Francis Thompson. His poems, which are full of gnomic wisdom, became extremely popular after his martyrdom for treason. On his return to England in 1586 he had become the secret chaplain to the Countess of Arundel, and exceeded the limit of forty days' residence in England for native-born Catholics. He was discovered in 1592, imprisoned, tortured and put to death three years later. His poem "The Burning Babe" was greatly admired by Ben Jonson. Many of his poems are extravagant in their search for figures, which are to be excused by the poet's religious fervour. The two poems included are classic in their terseness, polish and lucid moral statement. The texts are taken from A. B. Grosart's private edition of the *Complete Poems* (1872), many being from MSS. in Stoneyhurst College, Lancashire. Two volumes of Southwell's verse were published after his death in 1595.

TYMES GOE BY TURNES

MOST of Southwell's poems were written in prison between 1592 and 1595, many in the form of Complaints, the longest being the one "To St. Peter" secretly published in London by friends in 1595. Grosart describes the style of the ballad-like lyrics as "well-languaged" and "thought-packed". Southwell's latest biographer, Christopher Devlin, supports Grosart in believing that Shakespeare had read the manuscript poems when he was writing *Venus and Adonis, Lucrece* and *Love's Labour's Lost.* The purity of Southwell's un-Latinized English is due to the condensation of his sentences and the simplicity of his rhythms, dominated by syllables containing liquid consonants. The language is so clear and precise that it seldom needs glossing. In this poem the proverbial succinctness of the expression tends to a sequence of end-stopped lines. Southwell's habits of inversion and ellipsis are seen in lines 22 and 24 respectively; they are occasionally perplexing tricks of style.

> The loppèd tree in tyme may growe agayne;
> Most naked plants renewe both frute and floure;
> The soriest wight may finde release of payne,
> The dryest soyle sucke in some moystning shoure;
> 5 Tymes go by turnes and chaunces change by course,
> From foule to fayre, from better happ to worse.
>
> The sea of Fortune doth not ever floe,
> She drawes her favours to the lowest ebb;
> Her tide hath equall tymes to come and goe,
> 10 Her loome doth weave the fine and coarsest webb;
> No joy so great but runneth to an ende,
> No happ so harde but may in fine amende.
>
> Not allwayes fall of leafe nor ever springe,
> No endlesse night yet not eternall daye;
> 15 The saddest birdes a season finde to singe,
> The roughest storme a calme may soone alaye;
> Thus with succeeding turnes God tempereth all,
> That man may hope to rise yet feare to fall.

12 *in fine:* in the end.

A chaunce may wynne that by mischance was lost;
20 The nett that houldes no greate, takes little fishe;
In some thinges all, in all thinges none are croste,
Fewe all they neede, but none have all they wishe;
Unmedled joyes here to no man befall,
Who least hath some, who most hath never all.

23 *Unmedled:* unmingled.
24 *Who least hath some, who most hath never all:* i.e. The humblest have some (joys), the greatest never joy in everything.

LOSSE IN DELAYE

C. S. LEWIS thinks the gnomic poems of Southwell facile, and inferior to his novel attempts at a metaphysical style. Lines 13 to 16 of this poem contain a conceit, with something of what Grosart calls "pre-Raphaelite realism". The word *naked* (line 16) illustrates the weakness of some rhymes. The poem is a skilful versification of moral precepts, of which there are many examples in Elizabethan popular poetry. Southwell is an individualist; if he is influenced by any literary mode, it is that of Gascoigne.

Shunne delayes, they breede remorse;
    Take thy time while time doth serve thee;
Creepinge snayles have weakest force,
    Fly their fault lest thou repent thee.
5 Good is best when soonest wroughte,
Lingred labours come to noughte.

Hoyse upp sale while gale doth last,
    Tyde and winde stay no man's pleasure;
Seeke not tyme when tyme is paste,
10   Sober speede is wisdom's leysure.
After-wittes are deerely boughte,
Lett thy forewytt guide thy thoughte.

2 There is no need to emend *doth serve* to *is lent*, to make perfect the rhyme in line 4, as Turnbull did in his 1856 edition of the poems.
11 *After-wittes:* wisdom after the fact.
12 *forewytt:* foresight.

Tyme weares all his lockes before,
Take thy hould upon his forehead;
15 When he flyes he turnes no more,
And behinde his scalpe is naked.
Workes adjourn'd have many staies,
Long demurres breede new delayes.

Seeke thy salve while sore is grene,
20   Festred woundes aske deeper launcing;
After-cures are seldome seene,
Often sought scarsce ever chancinge.
Tyme and place give best advice,
Out of season, out of price.

25 Crush the serpent in the head,
Break ill egges ere they be hatched;
Kill bad chekins in the tredd,
Fligg, they hardly can be catched.
In the risinge stifle ill,
30 Lest it growe against thy will.

Droppes do perce the stubborne flynte,
Not by force but often fallinge;
Custome kills with feeble dinte,
More by use then strength prevayling.
35 Single sandes have little weighte,
Many make a drowninge freighte.

13 *Tyme weares all his lockes before:* Time personified appeared in Art
with his locks streaming out in front.

19 *grene:* uninfected, healthy.

22 *chancinge:* turning out effective.

24 *out of price:* without value.

26 *ill egges:* those that bring forth harmful birds or scorpions; for the
young scorpion has an egg-like casing.

27 *tredd:* conception.

28 *Fligg:* fledged.

33 *dinte:* stroke.

Tender twigges are bent with ease,
 Aged trees do breake with bending;
Younge desires make little prease,
40 Grouth doth make them past amendinge.
Happy man, that soone doth knocke
Babell babes againste the rocke!

39 *prease:* pressure, headway.
41-2 Grosart glosses: "Happy he that destroys wicked thoughts ere they
grow up." The reference to the babes of Babylon is found in *Isaiah*, xiii,
16.

Ben Jonson

TRUTH IS THE TRIALL OF IT SELFE

JAMES WARRE, to whom Jonson refers in line 17, was an unknown figure,
who apparently published in 1624 a book entitled *The Touchstone of Truth,
Wherein Veritie by Scripture Is Plainely Confirmed, and Errour Confuted.*
It contains this poem, with the initials B.J. subscribed. The composition
includes a number of biblical precepts, and the title-page of the book states
further that its purpose was to enable the reader "to argue with any Papist
and confute him by Scripture". Herford and Simpson took the text of the
poem from the Bodleian copy. The last two lines are unlike Jonson, and the
ascription of the poem to him is doubtful.

Truth is the triall of it selfe,
 And needs no other touch.
And purer then the purest Gold,
 Refine it neere so much.
5 It is the life and light of love,
 The Sunne that ever shineth,
And spirit of that speciall Grace,
 That Faith and Love defineth.
It is the Warrant of the Word,
10 That yeeld's a sent so sweete,
As gives a power to faith, to tread
 All false-hood under feete.

2 *touch:* test.

It is the Sword that doth divide
The Marrow from the Bone,
15   And in effect of Heavenly love
Doth shew the Holy one.
This, blessed Warre, thy blessed Booke
Unto the world doth prove.
A worthy worke, and worthy well
20   Of the most worthie love.

13 *It is the Sword, etc.:* The reference is to *Hebrews,* iv, 12.

Sir Henry Wotton

THE diversity and range of this great humanist's mind and character are reflected in the *Reliquae Wottonianiae* (1651), the admirable biography prefaced by Izaak Walton, and the tributes in verse and prose that appeared in the seventeenth century. He was born at Boughton Place, Maidstone, in 1568, and educated at Winchester and at New College and Queen's College, Oxford, where he became the friend of John Donne. At eighteen, he wrote a tragedy, *Tancredo,* that did not survive. At twenty, he completed his education by spending seven years on the Continent, mainly in France, Switzerland, Italy, Austria and southern Germany, where he made the acquaintance of several European humanists, including Casaubon and Sarpi, a connoisseur of art.

Wotton was employed on diplomatic missions, first by the Earl of Essex, and then by King James I, whom he represented at Venice for many years. He is said to have been sent to Scotland by Ferdinand, Grand Duke of Tuscany, to warn James of a plot upon his life by poisoning. But he had the misfortune to fall foul of his monarch by inscribing in Christopher Fleck-hammer's Common-Place Book at Augsberg, Germany, the definition: "An ambassador is an honest man sent *to lie* abroad for the good of his country." Conceived in English, this witty pun was comparatively harmless; but in Latin, the language in which the entry was made, the use of *mentire* could have only one connotation. The story is told in Logan Pearsall Smith's biography of Wotton, Vol. II. The abusive controversialist, Scioppius, quoted the epigram in an attack on James I's book against the Papacy, with the result that the King at a dinner demanded a public explanation of Wotton's indiscretion before the Court. In spite of two apologies, Wotton lost his employment in 1613, and was seriously in debt, relieved only by a pension from the Duke of Savoy.

In 1624 Wotton published his *Elements of Architecture.* It is said that Prince Charles, whose marriage he had been negotiating, pleaded for him to be made Provost of Eton in 1624. His wit and humour endeared him to his pupils, and he was so conscientious in fitting himself for his task that he took deacon's orders.

Though essentially a man of affairs, and a patron of letters, he wrote a number of memorable poems, moral in tone, a work called *The State of Christendom*, an unfinished *Survey of Education*, and a comparative study of the lives of Essex and Buckingham. His friendship with Walton was cemented by their common love of angling, which the Provost of Eton called "his idle time, not idly spent". He is mentioned with affection in several chapters of *The Compleat Angler*; and Walton says of his hospitality that, at table "his meat was choice, and his discourse better". A deeply religious man, Wotton was, in a distressed age, the most tolerant English gentleman in his attitude to the faith of others, as Walton shows in the anecdotes of his wise and witty exchanges with learned and quarrelsome contemporaries.

HOW HAPPY IS HE BORN AND TAUGHT

THE private morality that this poem reflects enabled Logan Pearsall Smith to date it. It must have been written in 1613 when Wotton was in disgrace; and was first published in 1614 in the fifth edition of Sir Thomas Overbury's didactic poem "The Wife". Professor Robert Birley reminds me that the poem is sung regularly as a hymn in College Chapel at Eton; it is perhaps the best statement of the humanist's credo that exists in English verse.

> How happy is he born and taught,
> That serveth not anothers will;
> Whose armour is his honest thought,
> And simple truth his utmost skill?
>
> 5 Whose passions not his masters are,
> Whose soul is still prepar'd for death;
> Unti'd unto the World by care
> Of publick fame, or private breath.
>
> Who envies none that chance doth raise,
> 10 Nor vice hath ever understood;

8 *private breath:* In a letter to Sir Dudley Carleton in 1613, Wotton wrote: "We learn hereafter to plant ourselves better than upon the grace or breath of men" (Logan Pearsall Smith).

How deepest wounds are giv'n by praise,
Nor rules of State, but rules of good.

Who hath his life from rumours freed,
Whose conscience is his strong retreat:
15   Whose state can neither flatterers feed,
Nor ruine make Oppressors great.

Who God doth late and early pray,
More of his grace than gifts to lend:
And entertain the harmless day
20   With a Religious Book, or Friend.

This man is freed from servile bands,
Of hope to rise, or fear to fall:
Lord of himself, though not of Lands,
And having nothing, yet hath all.

11-12 The construction of these lines is elliptical, for they should be preceded by some phrase, such as "Who knows . . ." The first half of line 12 would then read "Not rules of State". In other words, the happy man is he who governs his life by a private moral code, not the dictates of prudential policy. He is always wary of commendation, as likely to relax his strict self-discipline.

19 *the harmless day:* a transferred epithet, which should serve to modify "entertain".

21 *bands:* bonds.

Henry King

THE LABYRINTH

POETRY as religious pathos and reflection, in which the seventeenth century excelled other ages, takes different forms in King, Herbert, Vaughan and Crashaw. It starts with a belief in the vanity of this world (the refuge of a "sick soul") and ends with the grave as the repository of true wisdom. The function of meditation was to discover the other or disciplined self, a spiritual need induced by the uncertainty of an age in which thinking men groped for the meaning of life. They chose a spiritual pattern of living rather than remain at the mercy of their physical perceptions, which King here calls "a crooked Labyrinth" or "a perplexed circle". In stanza 2 he looks upon the unaided rational mind as vacillating between extremes of wrong decision and indecision or repentance.

Life is a crooked Labyrinth, and we
Are daily lost in that Obliquity.
'Tis a perplexed circle, in whose round
Nothing but sorrows and new sins abound.
5   How is the faint impression of each good
Drown'd in the vicious Channel of our blood?
Whose Ebbes and Tides by their vicissitude
Both our great Maker and our selves delude.

O wherefore is the most discerning eye
10 Unapt to make its own discovery?
Why is the clearest and best judging mind
In her own ills prevention dark and blind?
Dull to advise, to act precipitate,
We scarce think what to do, but when too late.
15 Or if we think, that fluid thought, like seed
Rots there to propagate some fouler deed.
Still we repent and sin, sin and repent;
We thaw and freeze, we harden and relent:
Those fires which cool'd to day, the morrows heat
20 Rekindles. Thus frail nature does repeat
What she unlearnt, and still by learning on
Perfects her lesson of confusion.

Sick soul! what cure shall I for thee devise,
Whose leprous state corrupts all remedies?
25 What medicine or what cordial can be got
For thee, who poyson'st thy best antidot?
Repentance is thy bane, since thou by it
Onely reviv'st the fault thou didst commit.
Nor griev'st thou for the past, but art in pain
30 For fear thou mayst not act it o're again.
So that thy tears, like water spilt on lime,
Serve not to quench, but to advance the crime.

26 *thy best antidot:* i.e. religion.
27-32 King holds an anti-Catholic view of the inefficacy of repentance;
he seems in the next stanza to prefer self-abasement of the sinner before
Christ.

My blessed Saviour! unto thee I flie
For help against this homebred tyrannie.
35   Thou canst true sorrows in my soul imprint,
And draw contrition from a breast of flint.
Thou canst reverse this labyrinth of sin
My wild affects and actions wander in.

O guide my faith! and by thy graces clew
40   Teach me to hunt that kingdom at the view
Where true joyes reign, which like their day shall last;
Those never clouded, nor that overcast.

38 *affects:* feelings, passions.

41 *like their day shall last:* the joy of faith being a perpetual illumination.

42 *Those never clouded, nor that overcast:* "Those" looks back to the joys of the Kingdom through faith; "that" refers to the Light of day through grace.

AN ELEGY OCCASIONED BY SICKNESS

KING says in one of his funeral sermons: "The Grave is commonly as powerful an Oratour as the Pulpit, and . . . instructs us in the Rules of a Good Life." These rules were held to be of divine origin, and to help man focus his consciousness upon life as a sacred trust, rather than a secular gift to be squandered. The melancholy introspection of this poem reflects King's state of mind after the loss of his wife, when he was seriously afflicted with illness.

Well did the Prophet ask, Lord what is man?
Implying by the question none can
But God resolve the doubt, much less define
What Elements this child of dust combine.

5   Man is a stranger to himself, and knowes
Nothing so naturally as his woes.
He loves to travel countreys, and confer
The sides of Heavens vast Diameter:

1 *what is man?:* The question is posed in the Old Testament both in the book of Job and by David in the *Psalms.* Presumably King regards either as a prophet.

2 *question:* a trisyllabic word in this context.   **7** *confer:* bring together.

Delights to sit in Nile or Boetis lap,
10 Before he hath sayl'd over his own Map;
By which means he returnes, his travel spent,
Less knowing of himself then when he went.
Who knowledge hunt kept under forrein locks,
May bring home wit to hold a Paradox,
15 Yet be fools still. Therefore might I advise,
I would inform the soul before the eyes:
Make man into his proper Opticks look,
And so become the student and the book.

With his conception, his first leaf, begin;
20 What is he there but complicated sin?
When riper time, and the approaching birth
Ranks him among the creatures of the earth,
His wailing mother sends him forth to greet
The light, wrapt in a bloudy winding sheet;
25 As if he came into the world to crave
No place to dwell in, but bespeak a grave.

Thus like a red and tempest-boading morn
His dawning is: for being newly born
He hayles th' ensuing storm with shrieks and cryes,
30 And fines for his admission with wet eyes.

How should that Plant whose leaf is bath'd in tears
Bear but a bitter fruit in elder years?
Just such is his; and his maturer age
Teems with event more sad then the presage.
35 For view him higher, when his childhoods span
Is raised up to Youths Meridian;
When he goes proudly laden with the fruit
Which health, or strength, or beauty contribute;

9-10 *Delights . . . Map:* i.e. loves to investigate the external world, before
he has studied himself.   *Boetis:* i.e. the Guadalquivir.
14 *a Paradox:* a different point of view.   16 *inform:* educate.
17 *into his proper Opticks look:* examine his own methods of observation.
20 *complicated sin:* the doctrine of Original Sin.
30 *fines:* pays a consideration for a special privilege.

     Yet as the mounted Canon batters down
40   The Towres and goodly structures of a town:
     So one short sickness will his force defeat,
     And his frail Cittadell to rubbish beat.
     How does a dropsie melt him to a floud,
     Making each vein run water more then bloud?
45   A Chollick wracks him like a Northern gust,
     And raging feavers crumble him to dust.
     In which unhappy state he is made worse
     By his diseases then his makers curse.
     God said in toyl and sweat he should earn bread,
50   And without labour not be nourished:
     Here, though like ropes of falling dew, his sweat
     Hangs on his lab'ring brow, he cannot eat.

     Thus are his sins scourg'd in opposed themes,
     And luxuries reveng'd by their extremes.
55   He who in health could never be content
     With Rarities fetcht from each Element,
     Is now much more afflicted to delight
     His tasteless Palate, and lost appetite.

     Besides though God ordain'd, that with the light
60   Man should begin his work, yet he made night
     For his repose, in which the weary sense
     Repaires it self by rests soft recompence.
     But now his watchful nights, and troubled dayes
     Confused heaps of fear and fancy raise.
65   His chamber seems a loose and trembling mine;
     His Pillow quilted with a Porcupine:
     Pain makes his downy Couch sharp thornes appear,
     And ev'ry feather prick him like a spear.
     Thus when all forms of death about him keep,
70   He copies death in any form but sleep.

     Poor walking clay! hast thou a mind to know
     To what unblest beginnings thou dost ow

43 *dropsie:* originally *hydropsy*; an accumulation of watery fluid in the
connective tissues, but not the veins, as King believes.

Thy wretched self? fall sick a while, and than
Thou wilt conceive the pedigree of Man.
75 Learn shalt thou from thine own Anatomie,
That earth his mother, wormes his sisters be:
That he's a short-liv'd vapour upward wrought,
And by corruption unto nothing brought:
A stagg'ring Meteor by cross Planets beat,
80 Which often reeles and falles before his set:
A tree that withers faster then it growes;
A torch puff't out by ev'ry wind that blowes;
A web of fourty weekes spun forth in pain,
And in a moment ravell'd out again.

85   This is the Model of frail man: Then say
That his duration's onely for a day:
And in that day more fits of changes pass,
Then Atomes run in the turn'd Hower-glass.

So that th'incessant cares which life invade
90 Might for strong truth their heresie perswade,
Who did maintain that humane soules are sent
Into the body for their punishment:
At least with that Greek Sage still make us cry,
Not to be born, or being born to dy.

95   But Faith steers up to a more glorious scope,
Which sweetens our sharp passage; and firm hope
Anchors our torne Barks on a blessed shore,
Beyond the Dead sea we here ferry o're.

73 *than:* then.

79 *A stagg'ring Meteor by cross Planets beat:* Meteors were inferior to the other heavenly bodies in astrology, and the planets could exercise malignant influence upon men. King likens man to a temporary illumination in the sky, struck down by a malignant ("cross") planet—a metaphysical conceit.

80 *set:* i.e. setting (falling to earth).

83 *fourty weekes:* referring to the period of gestation.

88 *Atomes:* minute particles.

90-2 The heresies are those of Origen (A.D. 185-253), philosopher and head of the Christian School in Alexandria, and Priscillian, a Gnostic mystic of Spain of the fourth century A.D.

93 *that Greek Sage:* probably Posidippus.

To this, Death is our Pilot, and disease
100   The Agent which solicites our release.

Though crosses then poure on my restless head,
Or lingring sickness nail me to my bed:
Let this my Thoughts eternall comfort bee,
That my clos'd eyes a better light shall see.
105   And when by fortunes or by natures stroke
My bodies earthen Pitcher must be broke,
My Soul, like Gideons lamp, from her crackt urn
Shall Deaths black night to endlesse lustre turn.

106-7 *Gideons lamp:* The reference is to *Judges*, vii, 16-20, which des-
cribes how Gideon and 300 men, provided with swords and lamps (con-
cealed in pitchers, subsequently broken), fell upon the host of the Midian-
ites at night, and put them to flight.

Sidney Godolphin

VAIN MAN, BORN TO NO HAPPINESS

SAINTSBURY describes this poem, from Harley MS. 6917 of the British
Museum, as a "Senecan chorus". The argument at first appears over-
subtle, especially lines 41-52. The frequently used word "sense" has a
different shade on each occasion. In view of the difficulties of Godolphin's
Christian Platonism, an interpretation is appended. The poem is included
for the dialectical management of its couplets; it is not metaphysical in its
use of images.

Vain man, born to no happiness,
But by the title of distress,
Allied to a capacity
Of joy, only by misery;
5   Whose pleasures are but remedies,
And best delights but the supplies
Of what he wants, who hath no sense
But poverty and indigence;
Is it not pain still to desire
10   And carry in our breast this fire?
Is it not deadness to have none,

7 *sense:* knowledge.

And satisfied, are we not stone?
Doth not our chiefest bliss then lie
Betwixt thirst and satiety,
15   In the midway: which is alone
In an half-satisfaction:
And is not love the middle way,
At which with most delight we stay?
Desire is total indigence,
20   But love is ever a mixt sense
Of what we have, and what we want,
And though it be a little scant
Of satisfaction, yet we rest
In such an half-possession best.
25   A half-possession doth supply
The pleasure of variety,
And frees us from inconstancy
By want caused, or satiety;
He never lov'd, who doth confess
30   He wanted aught he doth possess,
(Love to itself is recompense
Besides the pleasure of the sense)
And he again who doth pretend
That surfeited his love took end,
35   Confesses in his love's decay
His soul more mortal than that clay
Which carries it, for if his mind
Be in its purest part confin'd
(For such love is) and limited,
40   'Tis in the rest, dying, or dead:
They pass their times in dreams of love
When wavering passions gently move,
Through a calm smooth-fac'd sea they pass,
But in the haven traffic glass:

44 *traffic glass:* The verb *traffic* means "to trade in or barter", and must, I think, be taken literally. *Glass* may refer to the glass beads or baubles carried by traders to traffic with the natives. The word *glass* also looks back to the *smooth-fac'd sea*. The poet suggests how pedestrian the physical concept of love can become.

45 They who love truly through the clime
Of freezing North and scalding Line,
Sail to their joys, and have deep sense
Both of the loss, and recompense:
Yet strength of passion doth not prove
50 Infallibly, the truth of love.
Ships, which to-day a storm did find,
Are since becalm'd, and feel no wind.

46 *scalding Line:* the Equator.

INTERPRETATION OF THE POEM

THE happiness of men without sensibility is but the satisfaction of their animal wants (lines 1 to 8). But the gratification of desires merely leaves them where they were (9 and 10). To have none may be death; but to live for their gratification is to harden one's nature (11 and 12). Happiness is therefore a middle way between appetite and self-indulgence, and this choice is love (13 to 18). Physical desire betokens poverty of spirit; but true happiness is the ability to count one's blessings and to accommodate one's needs to one's meagre resources (19 to 24). This half-way house has the recompense of variety, and liberates us from the caprice caused by excessive wants and their regular gratification (25 to 28). No one loves life who hankers after what he cannot possess; for the good life has its own moral satisfactions, which the pleasures of the senses cannot supply (29 to 32). Anyone who pretends that love's satisfaction is its purpose must believe that the soul is more ephemeral than the body in which it is housed (33 to 37). Love is the purest aspect of mind; it may be limited in scope, but everything else it stands for is death (37 to 40). Those lovers are dreamers, who wait for passion to supply their motives; their destination reached, they become mere traffickers in the affections (41 to 44). True love is constant; whatever the emotional climate, one is aware both of the sacrifice and the gain (45 to 48). The truth of love lies not in the ardour of its passion, but in the patience to weather its storms, for the aftermath of peace of mind (49 to 52).

12. TOPOGRAPHICAL POEMS

JONSON'S "To Penshurst" is the first considerable poem of this type in English literature. Among classical authors the precursors of this kind are not many, the tendency being to generalize, rather than particularize, responses to natural surroundings. The poets after Hesiod and Homer had little sense of place, or of the country home as a seat of domestic culture. There was at Jonson's disposal George Chapman's Homer, with its description of Calypso's Island in the *Odyssey*, V. 51-83, and he may have read the seventh Idyll of Theocritus, which lovingly describes late summer in the country. In Latin the *Eclogues* and *Georgics* of Vergil, Catullus's verses on Sirmione, and Horace's *Odes*, *Epodes* (especially the second) and *Epistles*, with their recollections of his Sabine farm, may have come to mind; but the account of Sidney's hospitality in "Penshurst" rests mainly on *Martial*, III. 58.

In English, the topographical poem starts as a moral epistle, addressed to a place rather than a person. The finest long poems in this kind are "To Penshurst", Marvell's "Upon Appleton House" and Sir John Denham's "Cooper's Hill". Fine poetry, of similar reflections, was to come in the eighteenth century, in Pope's "Windsor Forest" and Goldsmith's "Deserted Village".

Ben Jonson

TO PENSHURST

THIS poem appeared in the miscellany known as *The Forrest*, published in the Jonson Folio of 1616. Penshurst, in Kent, was the country seat of the Sidney family, the head of which, at the time Jonson wrote, was Sir Robert, brother of Sir Philip Sidney. Waller, imitating Jonson, addressed a somewhat shorter appreciation to Penshurst later. T. S. Eliot wrote of Jonson: "Poetry of the surface cannot be understood without study. . . . The immediate appeal of Jonson is to the mind; his emotional tone is not in the single verse, but in the design of the whole." The truth of this is demonstrated in "To Penshurst", a cross-section of one aspect of Elizabethan life. With the peace, beauty and hospitality of nature itself, Jonson associates the moral worth of the Sidneys. It is their way of life he admires, its religious and educational value, not the palace they might inhabit. In the last couplet Jonson concludes that ostentatious houses are built for the proud, but simple domestic felicity is the mark of a home truly lived in.

Thou art not, Penshurst, built to envious show,
    Of touch, or marble; nor canst boast a row
Of polish'd pillars, or a roofe of gold:
    Thou hast no lantherne, whereof tales are told;
5 Or stayre, or courts; but stand'st an ancient pile,
    And these grudg'd at, art reverenc'd the while.
Thou joy'st in better markes, of soyle, of ayre,
    Of wood, of water: therein thou art faire.
Thou hast thy walkes for health, as well as sport:
10   Thy Mount, to which the Dryads doe resort,
  Where Pan, and Bacchus their high feasts have made,
    Beneath the broad beech, and the chest-nut shade;
That taller tree, which of a nut was set,
    At his great birth, where all the Muses met.
15 There, in the writhed barke, are cut the names
    Of many a Sylvane, taken with his flames.

2 *touch:* short for touchstone, a fine-grained quartz on which the quality of gold and silver alloys were tested by examining the colour of the streak. Other smooth, dark stones, such as marble or basalt, were often confused with it.

4 *lantherne:* originally a glassed-in room above the house itself, used as a solarium.

6 *grudg'd at:* secretly envied.

10 *Mount:* in the case of Penshurst, a hillock or elevated ground. *Dryads:* wood-nymphs.

11 *Bacchus:* son of Jupiter and Semele, god of the wine festival, vineyards and the cultivation of the earth. Most legends about him and his eternal youth are derived from the Egyptian god Osiris. He could inspire divine fury in musicians, and was usually clad in a panther skin and crowned with ivy and vine-leaves.

13-14 The reference is to the planting of a chestnut at the birth of Sir Philip Sidney on November 30, 1554. He became a celebrated poet, hence the allusion to the Muses.

16 *Sylvane:* spirit of the fields and woods, identified with Pan; here an admirer of Sir Philip Sidney—"taken with his flames", meaning "captivated by his poetic inspiration".

And thence, the ruddy Satyres oft provoke
    The lighter Faunes, to reach thy Ladies oke.
Thy copp's, too, nam'd of Gamage, thou hast there,
20   That never failes to serve thee season'd deere,
When thou would'st feast, or exercise thy friends.
    The lower land, that to the river bends,
Thy sheepe, thy bullocks, kine, and calves doe feed:
    The middle grounds thy mares, and horses breed.
25 Each banke doth yeeld thee coneyes; and the topps
    Fertile of wood, Ashore, and Sydney's copp's,
To crowne thy open table, doth provide
    The purpled pheasant, with the speckled side:
The painted partrich lyes in every field,
30   And, for thy messe, is willing to be kill'd.
And if the high-swolne Medway faile thy dish,

17 *the ruddy Satyres:* Greek demigods of the country, whose hairy bodies resembled men's, but hind quarters were those of goats. They were attendants on Bacchus in his orgies, and the first fruits of the summer were offered to them. They are called "ruddy" by Jonson, because usually depicted as flushed with wine.

18 *The lighter Faunes:* Jonson distinguishes these "mischievous goblins who induced nightmares" from Satyrs. But originally *Fauni* were simply the Roman version of the Greek *Satyri.* *Ladies oke:* According to Gifford, nineteenth-century editor of Jonson, the oak was named after Lady Leicester, who began her labour under this tree, presumably a little removed from the wood itself.

19 *Gamage:* Barbara Gamage, Sir Robert's wife, used to feed deer here.

25 *coneyes:* rabbits.

26 *Ashore, and Sydney's copp's:* The origin of the name of the first of these thickets is untraced.

27 *open table:* hospitable table, usually kept permanently laid.

28 *purpled pheasant:* Clothed in purple, the colour of royalty, originally deep red. The bird spread to western Europe from the river Phasis in Colchis, and is mentioned in English as early as the thirteenth century. The red variety may have been an importation from the Far East.

29 *painted partrich:* Jonson and most Elizabethan writers retained the mediaeval spelling for the bird: *painted* probably means "picturesque".

30 *messe:* originally a prepared dish or portion of food; the modern meaning dates only from the nineteenth century.

31 *Medway:* Tributary of the Thames that flows past Penshurst.

Thou hast thy ponds, that pay thee tribute fish,
Fat, aged carps, that runne into thy net.
  And pikes, now weary their owne kinde to eat,
35 As loth, the second draught, or cast to stay,
  Officiously, at first, themselves betray.
Bright eeles, that emulate them, and leape on land,
  Before the fisher, or into his hand.
Then hath thy orchard fruit, thy garden flowers,
40   Fresh as the ayre, and new as are the houres.
The earely cherry, with the later plum,
  Fig, grape, and quince, each in his time doth come:
The blushing apricot, and woolly peach
  Hang on thy walls, that every child may reach.
45 And though thy walls be of the countrey stone,
  They'are rear'd with no mans ruine, no mans grone,
There's none, that dwell about them, wish them downe;
  But all come in, the farmer, and the clowne:
And no one empty-handed, to salute
50   Thy lord, and lady, though they have no sute.
Some bring a capon, some a rurall cake,
  Some nuts, some apples; some that thinke they make
The better cheeses, bring 'hem; or else send
  By their ripe daughters, whom they would commend
55 This way to husbands; and whose baskets beare
  An embleme of themselves, in plum, or peare.
But what can this (more then expresse their love)
  Adde to thy free provisions, farre above

33-8 That the pike and eel are desperately anxious to be caught or netted is a conceit that illustrates the willingness of nature to help the generous husbandman.

36 *Officiously:* dutifully.

45-8 The notion of open hospitality is extended to the stone walls of the garden, which Jonson suggests were built without complaint, because of the goodness of those who dispensed the fruits of the gardeners' labours.

48 *the clowne:* the peasant.

50 *have no sute:* have no request, but come bringing their own humble gifts.

51 *capon:* emasculated poultry cock.

54 *ripe daughters:* mature, ready to be married.

The neede of such? whose liberall boord doth flow,
60   With all, that hospitalitie doth know!
Where comes no guest, but is allow'd to eate,
    Without his feare, and of thy lords owne meate:
Where the same beere, and bread, and selfe-same wine,
    That is his Lordships, shall be also mine.
65 And I not faine to sit (as some, this day,
    At great mens tables) and yet dine away.
Here no man tells my cups; nor, standing by,
    A waiter, doth my gluttony envy:
But gives me what I call, and lets me eate,
70   He knowes, below, he shall finde plentie of meate,
Thy tables hoord not up for the next day,
    Nor, when I take my lodging, need I pray
For fire, or lights, or livorie: all is there;
    As if thou, then, wert mine, or I raign'd here:
75 There's nothing I can wish, for which I stay.
    That found King James, when hunting late, this way,
With his brave sonne, the Prince, they saw thy fires
    Shine bright on every harth as the desires
Of thy Penates had beene set on flame,
80   To entertayne them; or the countrey came,
With all their zeale, to warme their welcome here.
    What (great, I will not say, but) sodayne cheare
Did'st thou, then, make 'hem! and what praise was heap'd
    On thy good lady, then! who, therein, reap'd

65 *faine:* obliged to; originally, "glad to", but the word changed its meaning in the sixteenth century.

66 *dine away:* eat elsewhere, because inadequately fed at the rich man's table.

67 *tells my cups:* counts my drinks.   **73** *livorie:* comforts.

74 i.e. as if we had exchanged positions in life.

75 *stay:* wait.

77 *the Prince:* Henry, Prince of Wales, who died in 1612.

79 *Penates:* household gods of the Romans, such as Vesta and the Lares, who blessed with fulness the storeroom. Their images were originally brought from Samothrace to Troy, and from there to Lavinium by Aeneas.

82 *sodayne cheare:* unsolicited and unpremeditated hospitality.

85   The just reward of her high huswifery;
      To have her linnen, plate, and all things nigh,
   When shee was farre: and not a roome, but drest,
      As if it had expected such a guest!
   These, Penshurst, are thy praise, and yet not all.
90   Thy lady's noble, fruitfull, chaste withall.
   His children thy great lord may call his owne:
      A fortune, in this age, but rarely knowne.
   They are, and have beene taught religion: Thence
      Their gentler spirits have suck'd innocence.
95   Each morne, and even, they are taught to pray,
      With the whole household, and may, every day,
   Reade, in their vertuous parents noble parts,
      The mysteries of manners, armes, and arts.
   Now, Penshurst, they that will proportion thee
100   With other edifices, when they see
   Those proud, ambitious heaps, and nothing else,
      May say, their lords have built, but thy lord dwells.

86-8 The suggestion is that Lady Sidney was absent when the King and Prince arrived, but that the best of everything was at all times ready for the unexpected guest.

93-8 Jonson praises the moral value of household worship, in which all members participate; also the importance of good parental example in a humanist education.

99 *proportion:* compare.

Thomas Carew

TO SAXHAM

MOST editors of Carew have noticed the resemblance of this poem to Jonson's tribute "To Penshurst". Carew is often regarded as a cynic and a sensualist; there is evidence here of some idealism. He was not a genuine humanist; his religious strain did not run as deep as his desire to emulate Jonson's craftsmanship. Little Saxham, near Bury St. Edmunds, was the country seat of Sir John Crofts, who died in 1628; Carew often stayed there as the friend of the younger John Crofts, who had also been in France in 1619 with Lord Herbert of Cherbury. The buildings were demolished in 1771. The poem seems to refer to a particular visit, made by Carew in the winter, possibly the Christmas season.

Though frost, and snow, lockt from mine eyes
That beautie which without dore lyes;
Thy gardens, orchards, walkes, that so
I might not all thy pleasures know;
5 Yet (Saxham) thou within thy gate,
Art of thy selfe so delicate;
So full of native sweets, that blesse
Thy roofe with inward happinesse;
As neither from, nor to thy store
10 Winter takes ought, or Spring addes more.
The cold and frozen ayre had sterv'd
Much poore, if not by thee preserv'd;
Whose prayers have made thy Table blest
With plenty, far above the rest.
15 The season hardly did afford
Course cates unto thy neighbours board,
Yet thou hadst daintyes, as the skie
Had only been thy Volarie;
Or else the birds, fearing the snow
20 Might to another deluge grow:
The Pheasant, Partiridge, and the Larke,
Flew to thy house, as to the Arke.
The willing Oxe, of himselfe came
Home to the slaughter, with the Lambe,
25 And every beast did thither bring
Himselfe, to be an offering.

11 *sterv'd:* a common spelling of *starved*; from Dutch, in which *sterven*, however, means "to die".

16 *Course cates:* ordinary home-made food. The words *course* and *coarse* were not distinguished in spelling until after 1700, though Izaac Walton used the modern adjectival form, apparently for the first time, in 1653.

18 *Volarie:* aviary.

21 *Partiridge:* metrically, a misspelling, but not an isolated one.

19-22 The image of the hungry flocks of birds "deluging" the Ark (Saxham) is in the nature of a metaphysical conceit.

23-30 The idea of the self-sacrificing beasts is clearly borrowed from Jonson's "To Penshurst". But the notion that three elements pay tribute to the fourth (fire) is Carew's own.

The scalie herd, more pleasure tooke,
Bath'd in thy dish, then in the brooke:
Water, Earth, Ayre, did all conspire,
30   To pay their tributes to thy fire,
Whose cherishing flames themselves divide
Through every roome, where they deride
The night, and cold abroad; whilst they
Like suns within, keepe endlesse day.
35   Those chearfull beames send forth their light,
To all that wander in the night,
And seeme to becken from aloofe,
The weary Pilgrim to thy roofe;
Where if refresh't, he will away,
40   Hee's fairly welcome, or if stay
Farre more, which he shall hearty find,
Both from the Master, and the Hinde.
The strangers welcome, each man there
Stamp'd on his chearfull brow, doth weare;
45   Nor doth this welcome, or his cheere
Grow lesse, 'cause he staies longer here.
There's none observes (much lesse repines)
How often this man sups or dines.
Thou hast no Porter at the doore
50   T'examine, or keep back the poore;
Nor locks, nor bolts; thy gates have bin
Made onely to let strangers in;
Untaught to shut, they doe not feare
To stand wide open all the yeare;
55   Carelesse who enters, for they know,
Thou never didst deserve a foe;
And as for theeves, thy bountie's such,
They cannot steale, thou giv'st so much.

27 *The scalie herd:* a periphrasis for "fish", which anticipates Pope.
31 *cherishing:* friendly.   **37** *aloofe:* afar.   **38** *Pilgrim:* wanderer.
39 *he will away:* he wishes to leave.   **42** *Hinde:* servant.
45 *cheere:* food and drink.
47-58 The gracious hyperbole of these lines suggests the munificence
of the hospitality, and is another of Carew's debts to Jonson.